A Nearly Normal Life

A Nearly Normal Life

a memoir

Charles L. Mee

LITTLE, BROWN AND COMPANY
BOSTON NEW YORK LONDON

The author is grateful for permission to include the following previously copyrighted
material:

Excerpts from *In the Shadow of Polio* by Kathryn Black. Copyright © 1996 by Kathryn
Black. Reprinted by permission of Addison Wesley Longman.

Excerpts from *Passage Through Crisis: Polio Victims and Their Families* by Fred Davis.
Copyright © 1991 by Fred Davis. Reprinted by permission of Transaction Publishers;
all rights reserved.

Excerpts from *Through the Storm: A Polio Story* by Robert F. Hall (North Star Press,
1990). Copyright © 1990 by Robert F. Hall. Reprinted by permission of the author.

Excerpts from *Polio's Legacy: An Oral History* edited by Edmund Sass. Copyright ©
1996 by University Press of America. Reprinted by permission of University Press of
America.

First Edition

Library of Congress Cataloging-in-Publication Data
Mee, Charles L.
     A nearly normal life : a memoir / by Charles L. Mee. — 1st ed.
        p.   cm.
     ISBN 0-316-55852-4
     1. Mee, Charles L. — Health. 2. Mee, Charles L. — Childhood and
youth. 3. Poliomyelitis — Patients — Illinois — Biography. I. Title.
RJ496.P2M526   1999
362.1'96835'0092 — dc21
     [b]   98-25245

10   9   8   7   6   5   4   3   2

MV-NY

Book design by Arlene Lee

Printed in the United States of America

For my children,
Erin, Charles, Sarah, and Alice

A Nearly Normal Life

one

It had never occurred to me that anything bad might happen to me. I was fourteen years old that summer of 1953, with buckteeth, a crew cut, a love of swimming, football, and comic books. I had a dog named Pat. I was a Boy Scout. I liked girls. I was just out of my freshman year in high school. This was in Barrington, Illinois, a little town, population 5,320, thirty-five miles northwest of Chicago. Where I lived in the village, you could walk to the end of the block and out into empty fields, rolling hills of tall grass; no one owned this land as far as we knew. It had little lakes where we would cut down saplings and build lean-tos and sometimes camp out overnight — no grown-ups, just the kids, boys and girls. My sister Bets, three years older than I, was one of the oldest of the kids; she was always my best friend, and with her, I knew I was always safe.

But parents lived in constant dread those days, especially in the summertime, fearful that their children might come down with polio. Polio struck suddenly, without warning, and left its victims dead, or paralyzed, washed up in wheelchairs, white-faced, shrunken, with frightened eyes, light blankets over their legs, or lying on their backs inside iron lungs — great heavy contraptions, like little one-man submarines, constantly shushing and hissing with the intake and exhaust of the air pressure that made a person's diaphragm expand and contract, breathing for him because the muscles in his chest had stopped working—his head and feet sticking out uselessly at either end.

Parents were crazed by this. There was no cure for polio, not even any reliable treatment. It could not be prevented. It triggered the sort of anxiety and frenzy and sorrow that have been set off in recent years by AIDS, or, long ago, by the bubonic plague. Medical researchers had known as far back as the turn of the twentieth century that polio was a virus. Later it was discovered that the virus entered the mouth, usually, traveled to the intestinal tract, and then invaded the nervous system. It was called poliomyelitis, I was told, because it stripped away from the nerves their myelin sheath, which acts like insulation around an electrical cord, so that the nerves short-circuited, sizzled, and died. They stopped sending signals to the muscles, and so the muscles stopped working. Arms and legs lay limp and useless. Some children with polio could no longer raise their heads off their pillows. Some could no longer breathe. But no one knew what to do about it.

And not everyone believed the medical researchers knew what they were talking about. There was a constant buzz about polio back then. One magazine article that summer said polio was related to diet. Another article said it was related to the color of your eyes. Kids at summer camp got it, and when a boy at a camp in upstate New York got it that summer, a health officer imposed a frantic quarantine and said no one would be let out of the camp till the polio season was over. There was a lot of it that year. The newspapers published statistics every week. As of the Fourth of July, the papers said, there were 4,680 cases in the United States—more than there had been by July 4 in 1952, which had been reckoned the worst year for polio in medical history. The final tally at the end of that year had been 57,628. Of course, none of these numbers were reliable; odd illnesses were added to the total, and mild cases went unreported. Someone said that public gatherings had been banned altogether in the Yukon. In Montgomery, Alabama, that summer the whole city broke out; more than 85 people caught it. An emergency was declared. In Tampa, Florida, a twenty-month-old boy named Gregory died of it; five days later, his eight-year-old sister, Sandra, died of it while their mother was in the delivery room giving birth to a new baby.

The rules were: Don't play with new friends—stick with your old friends, whose germs you already have; stay away from crowded beaches and pools, especially in August; wash your hands before eating; never use another person's eating utensils or toothbrush or drink out of the same glass or Coke bottle; don't bite another person's hands or fingers while playing, or (this one for small children) put another child's toys in your mouth; don't pick up anything from the ground, especially around a beach or pool; don't have any teeth pulled during the summer; don't get overtired or strained; if you get a headache, tell your mother.

Even so, kids caught it. In the big city hospitals, kids were stacked like cordwood in the corridors. Massachusetts General Hospital, it was said, looked like a "medieval pest house." Carts and wheelchairs clogged the aisles; sixty monstrous iron lungs had been jammed into one ward room. On the South

Side of Chicago, a mother cried just to see the name above the door of the place where her child was taken: the Home for Destitute Crippled Children.

Maybe the worst trauma I had suffered recently had been my father's insistence that now that I was out of grammar school, I needed to throw away my comic book collection. But even that blow had been tempered by my mother, who interceded to rescue the "Li'l Bad Wolf" series of comics, which she said were not bad for me.

My greatest passion was football. I'd played it since I was five or six, with the certain assumption that I would be a college player, maybe a professional. The best college team in the country then was Notre Dame, and my father had a friend, an automobile dealer, who had a friend who was friends with Notre Dame's athletic director, Moose Krause. So, three times in my growing-up years, we drove to South Bend, Indiana, to see Notre Dame play. These were the days when Frank Leahy was the coach. It's hard to imagine what that name meant to a football-playing boy in the Midwest. Michael Jordan. Arnold Schwarzenegger. Obi Wan Kenobe. I remember going into the locker room before a game against Michigan State and seeing piles of hundreds of jerseys. Each player had several dozen jerseys with his number on them, and it was explained to me that these were tear-away jerseys, so that if a tackler got hold of nothing but your shirt, it would just come off in his hands, and you'd be gone. My plan was to play quarterback for Notre Dame, and I was encouraged to believe — by Frank Leahy and Moose Krause and the coaches back home — that this was not impossible.

My father didn't discourage this ambition, but he was a man who wore a three-piece suit and bifocals with thin silver rims. He shined his shoes and put shoe trees in them every night. Handsome, dignified, graying at the temples, he was unfailingly gracious and considerate (my mother said a gentleman always considered not simply another person's rights but also her preferences), as well as short-tempered and given to sudden rage if another driver pulled out in front of him so that he had to call the bastard a stupid son-of-a-bitch. My father was a businessman, at that time a vice president of the Commonwealth Edison Company of Chicago, and he believed in the promise of technology. In those days, when Ronald Reagan appeared in television commercials for General Electric and said, "Progress is our most important product," my family agreed with him.

We had driven cross-country that summer to Colorado, where my sister Sookie, five years older than I, was finishing her junior year at the University of Colorado at Boulder. Well, Bets and my mother and I drove out; my father took a plane out and back because he was busy at the office. My mother was a timid driver. She was the baby of her family. Her older sister, Douga, had gone to New York to be an actress, and instead became one of the stars of radio, among the inventors of the early-morning talk show. Douga met and married the founder and publisher of *Yachting* magazine, and the two of them lived in a triplex on Park Avenue, just like New Yorkers. But my mother was shy and tender. And I always felt, as the baby of *my* family, that she and I knew each other intimately, without a need for words: we were always close.

It took several days to get to Boulder, driving through the cornfields and the wheat fields of Iowa and Nebraska and on into the tornado lands of Dorothy's Kansas, staying in small motels along the way. This was the first time I'd gone farther out into the world than to South Bend, and I was excited to see other people's lives and wonder about how they lived them. My friend Dave's grandfather, Grampa Buckley, who had a seat on the Chicago Grain Exchange, used to drive out this way a couple of times a year to look at the fields. He would get out of his car and talk to the farmers, walk out into the corn and wheat and soybeans and feel the crops with his own fingers. This was how he discovered one year that the soybean crop was going to be a disaster—and the coming shortage of soybeans would drive their price sky-high at harvesttime. As he went from town to town, he would call back to his office in Chicago and say, "Buy soybeans, buy soybeans," until he cornered the market that year in soybeans.

This country, in the fifties, was the most wholesome country history has ever seen. Of course there were no drugs in schools, and no guns. For a girl to get pregnant in high school—as one did in Barrington—was a major community event. The child's father was a star on the high school basketball team, the president of the Honor Society, a bright boy with a promising future. The mother was a cheerleader, and a bright girl with a promising future. The town's consensus was that the girl should drop out of school right away to prepare for the birth, and the boy should be allowed to finish his junior year in high school and then get a job to support his family, which is what they did. When the child was three years old, the mother got a job at the checkout counter at the Jewel Tea supermarket.

Driving cross-country, across a country distinctly intact—in such sharp contrast to all the photographs of war-ravaged Europe that had recently filled the minds of growing children—a boy could be forgiven for having a sense of the everlasting peace and prosperity that President Eisenhower liked to talk about. We drove through small towns that had not changed in decades. Wherever new houses had been built, they were ranch houses, with vast picture windows on their fronts. Imagine feeling safe enough to put nothing but a sheet of glass between yourself and the world. In the Middle Ages, as in most periods of history, people built homes with walls two feet thick, massive bolted doors, ironwork over the windows. But in these past ten thousand years, for a period of about twenty years, so secure did an entire nation of people feel that they opened themselves up with complete vulnerability to anyone who had a rock. This is how safe we felt we were in the fifties, how safe I felt driving cross-country with my mother and Bets.

I thought of Sookie, the eldest of the three of us children, the way Winston Churchill said he thought of his mother: "She was like the evening star. She loved me dearly, but at a distance." Sookie was glamorous to me. I'm talking about a college girl from the Midwest, but she seemed immensely sophisticated to me, and she was dating a guy at the University of Colorado who wanted to be a professional golfer. My father thought he was a bum, and I guess he was, but he was a good-looking guy, maybe a little too slick, and very cool, the way natural athletes are, with their loose-limbed, easy way of moving. I tried to imitate him.

That may have been where I picked up the virus — in Boulder, or somewhere along the road to Boulder, in Kansas or Nebraska, from a water glass in a roadside diner, or a doorknob at a motel. I don't know. No one knows. But the incubation period is about fourteen days, and it was fourteen days after we arrived in Boulder, when I was back home in Barrington, that I came down with what felt like the flu, but not quite: an ache, a general sense of unease, a little light-headedness, that whiting out around the edges of my vision that I noticed first in the sun at the swimming pool where I was that afternoon. My lower back felt as though it needed stretching out. I thought maybe I'd pulled a muscle diving off the high board. For a while I lay beside the pool, waiting for the ache and tiredness to go away, but, feeling restless, I got up again and went home to lie down out of the sun in the coolness of the living room.

That night I had a date, finally, with Stephanie Sibley for a high school summer dance. There was to be dinner and swimming. A local country club had let the students use its clubhouse, and there would be an evening of wandering out onto the veranda, strolling out onto the golf course—like a black-and-white movie from the thirties. She had gotten a for-mal dress. I had rented a tuxedo with a white jacket. I was anx-ious about my date, but nothing else, not wanting to be sick so I couldn't go.

By the time I picked up Stevie—an older friend was double-dating with me, and drove—I was working hard to be relaxed and casual and happy. I told her I didn't feel well; I didn't want her to catch whatever it was I had. She laughed and said she didn't care. In the parking lot at the club, I felt dizzy. En-tering the club, I would have felt self-conscious and out of place, intimidated by the doorman, but my attention was too narrowly focused, by now, on how unsteady I felt on my feet. This began to seem strange to me, but so strong is the dating instinct for an adolescent boy that I repressed any thought that I was sick.

A buffet dinner was set out in the club's large dining room—little hors d'ouevres, a vast salmon lying stretched out on the table, I don't know what. I was hungry and ill at the same time. I took something in my fingers and looked for a place to put it down. Stevie had gone somewhere. I sat down, my head between my knees.

And then we danced. A vast ballroom, all white, with a crystal chandelier, great windows on two sides overlooking the outdoor swimming pool, all lit up and alive with teenage boys and girls, and the eighteenth green at the edge of the darkness. I could hardly stand. Weak in the knees. Rubbery.

Going for a swim was out of the question. To think of it made me shiver. We went down to the pool, where some of the kids had brought out some Scotch to drink. I couldn't stomach it. I was beginning to panic. A girl was pushed into the pool with her dress on. Some boys were thrown in with their tuxedos on; others jumped in fully clothed. Much laughter. Good times. I needed to go. The fear had begun to overtake me — deep down somewhere in the reticular activating system of the brain, some danger signals were going off, telling me that this was not a previously recognized sort of sickness — but I fought it off.

Our double-dating foursome drove back to Stevie's house, which had a rec room in the basement — a private place for teenagers in the fifties, if they had permissive, not to say lascivious, parents: a cozy paneled room with easy chairs, a couch, Coke in a refrigerator, a phonograph. Elvis had only just begun to play the guitar; Bill Haley and the Comets were about to record "Rock Around the Clock." The rec room was where I had imagined, for more than a year, that I would first kiss Stevie. At the top of the basement stairs, I stopped — aware, suddenly, that I was about to fall headfirst down the stairs. Holding the railings on both sides, I took a step down.

My knees turned to jelly. The others, already at the bottom of the stairs, looked up with concern. I said I had to go home. The other boy came back up the stairs and held me while I turned around and got back up to the top. He said he would give me a ride home, but I said no, I would walk, I was fine— needed a little fresh air, that was all. I don't think I said good night to Stevie. I felt nothing so much as humiliation. This night was the beginning, and the end, of my adolescent entry into the world of sex and the transition to adult love. My rite of passage into grown-up love would have to be scattered messily through my twenties and even thirties, a moment of transition returned to again and again before I got it quite right.

They watched me go out the door and stagger across Stevie's front lawn. I was maybe fifteen blocks from home. And I don't remember the walk home well. These were small-town suburban blocks, brick and wood frame houses from the twenties and thirties mostly, some new ranch houses with big lawns both front and back; I knew just which back yards I could cut through.

I fell down many times, weaving through these familiar yards. Sometimes I thought I would not be able to get back up. Once when I fell, I stayed down for a long time, thinking I would nap and recover my strength. I was shivering. It was a warm summer night, but I had some unreasoning fear I would die of exposure. This no longer seemed like the flu, but it was not like anything I knew either. Any boy's mother or father would have recognized these symptoms right away in those days, but I was not a mother or father; I was a growing boy oblivious to the possibility that some dread disease might strike *me*.

At home, I crawled up the stairs on my hands and knees to my room, my parents calling out from their room to ask if I was all right. I reassured them. But then I couldn't stay in bed. My legs hurt so, and were so restless. I walked up and down the hall. The light went on in my parents' room. I went back to bed. Both my mother and my father came to my door. I told them how I felt—a little nausea, the relentless aching in the legs, the weakness. They phoned Doc Welch, the kind of guy in those days who made house calls in the middle of the night. He said we should meet him at the hospital. This was three or four o'clock in the morning.

My father backed the car out of the garage. I lay across the back seat, with a kitchen pot at hand in case I needed to vomit. The hospital was eighteen miles away, past farms in the countryside, past cornfields and woodlots, through the kinds of hills where we had built our lean-tos, to Elgin, a little town big enough to have a hospital, Sherman Hospital.

We were met at the door of the emergency room by a flurry of nurses and orderlies with a wheelchair—and because, by this time, I could no longer walk, I was lifted into the chair, and we made our way, this little band of panic, nurses and orderlies in their noisy, rustling, starched white uniforms, through the disinfected corridors, into the elevator, up into another, nearly deserted, wing of the hospital, and down a darkened hall to an examining room, where a single light was found and turned on, so that deep shadows filled the corners of the room. The orderlies lifted me onto a high table, and the crowd of nurses parted to let an immense red-haired woman, the head nurse, step forward, look at me lying on the table, and pronounce without hesitation: "This boy has polio."

two

All the others stepped back, away from me; and the redheaded woman, strong as a linebacker for the Green Bay Packers, lifted me up in her arms—while the others who had touched me stepped to the sink one at a time and washed their hands.

The redheaded nurse carried me out of the examining room and back down the corridor, through swinging double doors, into the immense quiet of the isolation ward.

As she carried me into the solitude, all the while talking to me about her boys, both professional football players, and we turned left into an empty room, where she laid me in an empty bed, I understood that she was running the risk of contagion and death holding me, carrying me in her arms. A brave, heroic woman. I understood it the moment she picked me up. Mrs. Fuller was her name. Elgin, Illinois. July 1953.

And I felt a shudder of deep, deep fear; I felt an abyss open up beneath me, and, as far as I knew, there was no bottom to it; I felt awesome terror. Now the half-remembered stories flooded in on me, fragments of barely noticed newspaper reports and overheard conversations about polio outbreaks at summer camps, kids on crutches and in iron lungs. Now I understood: It had happened to me. And in an instant I got the whole picture, that this was a matter of my own life or death; that I needed to summon up everything I had—whatever that might be—to survive. I was, in that moment, separated from the rest of the world. My mother and father and Mrs. Fuller and others might want to help me. But I had just crossed over into a world unknown to them, where they could not follow me the whole way.

Placed in bed, I was alone. Mrs. Fuller disappeared, to call the doctor, she said, to set things in motion for my care. I never saw Doc Welch, and now I supposed I'd been delivered into the hands of people who specialized in polio. In any case, I was consumed by just how sick I felt now, this combination of nausea, pain, and cold fear. The occasional nurse came and went quickly, to bring a pitcher of water or to take my temperature without a word—frightened to be in the same room with me. Several hours later that morning, my parents, shrouded in white gowns, with white masks over their mouths and noses, were allowed to come just inside the door to let me see them, to know that they were there; and then they were urged out again.

In mid-morning, a doctor I had never met came into the room accompanied by a couple of nurses and interns and rolled me over on my side, explaining to me that they needed to take a sample of spinal fluid from my back to make sure of my diagnosis. Before I was rolled over, I caught a glimpse of the needle, which was terrifyingly long; surely they had made some mistake, surely this was a veterinarian's needle, meant for horses. I was afraid it would go all the way up into my brain. Several of them held me down, and bent me double. There was not much pain from the needle; there was only fear, along with dread of the expected confirmation of polio.

I thought: Things happen so suddenly in life, things that, in an instant, transform a life forever. You grow up thinking you can always say: no, I didn't mean that; I take it back. But this is not always the case.

With the drawing of the sample of spinal fluid, the doctor's work was finished. He could do nothing more but wait, to see whether or not I would come through. My parents, my sisters, the nurses: all any of them could do was wait.

The isolation ward was well named: I have never been so alone in my life as in that bed, where I was confined for the next three weeks, feverish and contagious; where I would learn, thoroughly, the lesson of self-reliance. It was an education that would sustain me for the rest of my life — and cut me off from others so that, even today, I have to work to remember that what I learned so well was wrong, or incomplete.

And somewhere deep inside I turned tough as old leather for ten or fifteen years. Or maybe I should say, more exactly, that whatever I felt from this time on, whatever fear or loneliness or sense of abandonment or, in the days to come, whatever thought of how unequal I was to the task, whatever sorrow or bitterness, whatever sense of longing or loss — all these would be merely superficial emotions laid on top of a profound and abiding rage: to survive. No feeling was as powerful as that one. And no feeling would be allowed to get in the way of that one, to put that passion in second place.

It is true what Samuel Johnson said: that the prospect of hanging wonderfully concentrates the mind. It reveals to us, in an instant, knowledge we didn't know we had; it teaches us lessons in a moment that might otherwise have taken a lifetime to learn; it throws us onto resources we never imagined we possessed, even if we are just children. And it turns out that human creatures are a very resilient species; all of us have re-serves we hardly ever use. It turns out that we can withstand a lot of damage; we can endure a long time; our systems are im-mensely rugged; we are as tough as cockroaches, really.

No feeling—of fear or sorrow or loneliness or loss—was indulged if it invited me to wallow in it, linger in it, settle into it, sink in it. In the moments that the fear diminished, I could feel the sadness well up in me. But sadness is an emotion about the past, and a longing for the past had just become, for me, a luxury I could not allow myself. I had no use for sadness—sadness could overwhelm me; sadness could immobilize me; sadness could kill me. And whenever I felt it, I fought it off.

Denial is an underrated ability these days; but billions of years of evolution gave it to us for a good reason, up to a point. It allows us to keep the bad news and the overpowering feelings at a distance, and then, later on, let them in just a bit at a time, just as much as we can take, bit by bit, until we've absorbed them all without letting them overcome us. So shocking was this trauma to me that it would be years before I could let such things as sorrow flow back into my life freely.

And, as it turned out, I hadn't received all the bad news yet anyway. The virus was not finished with me. It had only started. In the next two weeks, in the summer heat, delirious from fever, I went from a healthy athletic boy weighing 160 pounds to a frightened child of 90 pounds, unable to move a muscle except for three fingers of my left hand, not knowing where it would all end.

As the neurons in my body died one by one during those two weeks, I felt relentless pain, like the pain of a tooth being drilled without novocaine, but all over my body. As though a dentist was peeling back my skin, layer by layer, exposing each neuron individually, taking hold of each one with a pair of tweezers, and drilling down the length of it to its root, until he had burned it out. Then starting again, peeling back another layer of flesh, burrowing deeper into my body, going down inside the bone, as I sank deeper and deeper into delirium, surfacing only partly from time to time when some white-clad figure moved through my room.

I was not given any painkiller; I was told that pain medication might somehow cause additional damage.

I had read somewhere that an Olympic decathlon champion, Bob someone, who had had rheumatic fever as a child, had gone to bed each night and practiced relaxing his body part by part, starting with his toes, working slowly up his body all the way to his scalp, and then starting over again, from toes to scalp over and over again. I did the same, relaxing into the pain, not resisting it, feeling each neuron flare, scream, and die. I thought: From now on I can face anything.

When the fever subsided from time to time and I rose to some state near consciousness, I lay in bed, studying the ceiling. I could move my eyes enough to see an edge of the window, but I could not turn my head, so I could not see out into the sky. We are all trapped inside our bodies, but fourteen-year-old boys don't know this. For me, when the conditions of imprisonment suddenly changed in the summer of '53, my mind simply left my body, and it never came back for good. My sense of who I am would never again reside in a body that let me down; it moved instead into a mind that promised to be more trustworthy, more devious and elusive; that can escape when it needs to; that still, today, lives in a realm where it can take flight; that cannot not be pinned down; that refuses to place its faith or trust in the material world. We all know our mind and our body are two separate things: for me, that awareness is present now every moment of my life. I'm not crazy; I don't have multiple personalities; but I do know that the body I move around and put here and there in the world is something separate from my self. And sometimes I still want to hurt it for what it did to me, to take revenge against it, to let its aches and pains go unnoticed and untreated.

At night, I could hear a man down the hall crying out: "Oh, no, please. Don't. Oh, please, don't. No, oh, no, please."

He went on like that for several hours every night. Finally, I realized it was not my own dream. I asked a nurse what it was. She said a man had burned himself all over his body. All his skin was gone. And even the touch of the sheets was so painful it made him cry out. They gave him morphine, but she said they were afraid to give him too much. And, in any case, they were running short of good veins, ones that had not been punctured too many times with needles.

Time slowed to a drift. There were no events outside my own body to orient me to the world's news, family activities, the passing of the day or night — just this endless drift inside myself, with the occasional sound, the opening or closing of a door, the impression of something white and starched going quickly past my bed, the rush of water in the sink, the awareness that it was nighttime in the room.

I could blink, and I could breathe. I could make sounds. Had there been anyone in the room with me, I could have talked, though I'm sure not very coherently. And finally I conceived of a strategy: As long as I could keep breathing, I would not die. So I concentrated on my breathing, keeping it regular, not stopping. I imagined there was a place somewhere deep inside me that refused to die, and I relied on that place.

All about me, the people who would have ministered to me, would have helped me if they could, who would have done something for me had there been anything to do, stood waiting.

In some polio wards, the children lay awake at night, their eyes wide open, listening to the night sounds, unable to sleep, not knowing the reason they lay awake was that polio often caused encephalitis, an inflammation of the brain that kept the mind alert at night and drowsy during the day.

As I lay in bed at night, I monitored my body, thinking: I've lost all sense of myself, all sense of arms and legs and torso, all sense of fingers, all sense of anything but ferocious pain, but this body doesn't feel yet as though it is dying; it doesn't feel as though it can't breathe so that it will need to be sealed up inside an iron lung; I may have found some plateau where I can hold my own.

Then one night I saw my friends come through the door. They had been out driving around and stopped by to pick me up and take me out for a Coke. I thought I couldn't go, but they laughed and said for sure I could, and then they would bring me back. Oddly enough, Bill Dow was there. He wasn't a good friend of mine—I was surprised he had come by—but he had a certain standing with a certain group of guys, some cool guys, big dogs; to hang out with him meant a certain acceptance into that certain group. So, with strength I didn't know I had, somehow I pulled myself up and threw myself out of bed and down onto the floor. There I awoke, in a way. The friends were gone. Instead I was balanced delicately way out in outer space, on a dozen or so brightly colored discs, some of them two or three feet in diameter, the thickness of dinner plates. My job was to keep them in perfect harmony, by shifting my weight one way and another, so that they didn't spin out of control and fly off and leave me alone somewhere in the stars. Just then a night nurse came into my room, saw me on the floor, assumed that I was dead, screamed, and ran out. I thought that was odd. I tried to call out for help, but I could tell I wasn't making much of a sound.

After what seemed like a long while, a little gaggle of orderlies and interns came into the room to remove the body, and found — to their astonishment — that I was still alive. They worked a sheet underneath me on the floor and lifted me back onto the bed. And then they put guardrails all around the bed to keep me from getting out again — which seemed balmy to me, since by that time I knew I had used up every last reserve of strength in my effort to escape.

To pacify me, and because my mother was so quietly and patiently insistent, the hospital administrator allowed my parents to visit me the next day and then, from time to time in the days that followed, to step just inside the door in white masks and gowns, and let me know they were there.

A priest arrived to give me extreme unction, the last rites in the Roman Catholic church. I had been raised a Catholic, and I expected one day to be given extreme unction. But this seemed, even to my feverish mind, awfully hasty on the part of the church. I decided at once, as soon as the priest said he was going to give me extreme unction, that if the church was going to write me off, then I was going to write it off, too. And in that instant, I became an ex-Catholic. I thought: In my time of need, in the one moment of my life so far that I need the greatest help, does the church offer to pray for me night and day, with every ounce of strength, never letting go, never giving up, bringing every resource it has to praying that I live?

No. It lets me go without the smallest effort. Its goal was — as, in fact, it had always said — to get me to heaven, not to keep me alive on earth. In that instant, the Catholic church became an impediment to my survival, and I dropped it without the breath of a hesitation and with a deep, bitter hatred.

But I didn't want to hurt this priest's feelings. He had come a long way, the eighteen miles from Barrington to Elgin, to do what he thought he could for me. Father Thane. An elderly man, bald, with a ring of white hair like a tonsure. Not a man who was trying to do bad things in the world. I had served Mass for him many times. He asked me if I had anything I'd like to confess. Was he kidding? Anything to confess? I suppose I had expected the question, but I did think Father Thane had lost his bearings here a little bit about who was sinned against and who was sinning. Such anger surged up in me toward this good man that I was frightened by the savagery of it. Still, I replied politely, remembering who he was, not wanting to upset his routine: No, thank you, I said, I don't think so. He recited a few prayers — too quiet for me to hear, more for his benefit than mine. He did not anoint me with holy oils. I imagine he was afraid to touch me.

I have to say here, as painful as it is for me to say it, that I knew it would have been my devoutly Catholic father who had called the priest to give me the last rites. And so, although he was doing the best he knew, I experienced it as my father writing me off, too, or at least hedging his bets. And I didn't recover from that act until, maybe, a half-dozen years before his own death at the age of ninety-four. By then, we were very close again, comfortable with each other, able to sit quietly together for hours with only a word or two to convey a perfect understanding, and I often thought one of the greatest gifts he ever gave me was to live long enough for me to get back to him again.

An hour or so after the priest had given me extreme unction, my high school football coach came in to visit, stood far back against the wall, as far away from me as he could get, and told me I looked great, he was sure I'd be up in no time and back playing football in the fall. He said the team was counting on me. For a fleeting moment, I thought I might be hallucinating again. I was still in terrible, distracting, disorienting pain. The coach said that I might miss some of the early practices, so he would send over the playbook for me to study the new plays he had designed for that season. And as I listened to him, I realized: There will be people who will lie to me now, to keep my spirits up. Suddenly, I wanted to lash out at this man for lying to me—but of course, I could not, literally, lash out at anyone. I had never been a boy who lashed out at people. But now that I couldn't, I really wanted to. And so, instead, I tried a judo trick. I tried to master my feelings with strong understanding, so that I would no longer want to do what I couldn't do.

I thought: Anger is a waste of valuable energy. And more than that, I have something to learn here: that from now on, it is up to me to know the truth even if no one tells it to me. It's important for me to know that for my survival. That's where my energy needs to go.

And so I lied to the football coach in return: I thanked him, and said yes, I was sure I'd be back for fall practice. I wasted no energy arguing with him—what was the point?— and anyway, he wasn't a bad guy. He was only trying to cheer me up.

Still, this exercise in understanding took a toll on me right from the beginning, even in my first few efforts at it. I was, after all, only a fourteen-year-old kid, who had had no lessons in this art of emotional judo and was not getting it so perfectly right away—sometimes overreacting, seeing a mortal threat where I could just have relaxed. I couldn't tell where the threats were coming from, what things endangered my life, where I might have been better off just feeling bad and going where the current took me. My instincts were off.

Where I drew the line, finally, on being understanding was at the scapular medals that were being put all over my body. My mother and father, who were in a state of deep grief and hysteria, hired private nurses for me after I had been in the isolation ward for several days. These nurses were with me around the clock, taking some of the sting out of the sense of seclusion, doing as much as anyone could for me, giving me water to drink, putting damp cloths on my forehead to cool my fever. They were brave women. Not all nurses by any means were willing to take polio patients. These women came straight from the tradition of the Hippocratic oath and Florence Nightingale. They risked their lives for children in pain and anguish. But one of the nurses, a devout Catholic, brought holy medals and scapular medals with her every night. Every night, the number of holy medals ringing the periphery of my body increased. I was coming to feel like a dead Spanish saint. As hard as I tried, I hadn't the strength in either arm to brush these things away. I thought: If I let people prepare me for death, I will die. And again, I thought: This is a good woman, doing all she can think to help me; she has been hired by my parents, who are doing all they can think to help me. But this good woman is preparing me for a coffin. She is going to stop me from breathing. I thought: If I try to put an end to this, it will offend my father deeply. But, finally, I asked my father to fire the nurse and to take away the holy medals. And of course—though he was surprised by my request—he did it right away.

I have heard other people say that when they were in the isolation ward with polio, their parents were not allowed to visit them at all. That their parents had to stand behind a glass, like the window in a maternity ward, to look at their children. Later on, I would hear someone say that the only person who ever came to visit was his mother. And one day, she moved his bed over to the window, and for the first time, he realized that he was far above the ground, even above the trees. He turned his head to see where his mother pointed, and there were his father and brother and sister, looking up and waving—and it was at that moment that he felt for the first time the sense of deep alienation that would never leave him. Later on, his father came into the room to visit instead of his mother, and he had the boy get out of bed, to see if he could stand up yet, which, of course, he could not do.

Another child was not allowed to see his mother because she was pregnant at the time, and the doctor was afraid she would miscarry if she was exposed to the polio virus. The boy's only visits were from his father—just ten minutes every Sunday, his father standing behind a glass to keep from getting sick himself. This boy didn't see his mother from October to March, when she came straight from the maternity hospital after delivering his sister.

Some people I meet these days who had polio back when I did remember almost nothing. They've repressed it all, slammed it shut forever. Some have fragmented memories: some moments are vivid, others are gone. They remember as much as they can bear, or as much as they allowed themselves to take in or to feel at the time. Some people remember the rattle of food carts in the hallway, distant bells, elevator doors opening and closing, a sudden rush of sound as the door to the room opens and closes, letting in the harsh sharp noises of the corridor to the nurses' station. The dominant odor was of disinfectant. The dominant taste was of alcohol-disinfected thermometers. The occasional scent of perfume from a nurse leaning over to tuck in a sheet. The scent of my own sweat as I lay in a pool of it, the back of my neck damp. The haze of white everywhere: my own body shrouded in white gown and white sheets, nursed by women in white surgical masks, their white dresses starched to the smooth brittleness of Communion wafers. The dreadful silence, broken by the faint whispers of medical conversations on the far side of the drawn white curtains, the quiet *shush* of soft-soled nurses' shoes, and the ever-present sound of water in a basin, the ceaseless washing of hands.

But everyone I know has one memory vivid above all others: the sound of their mother's high-heeled shoes in the hallway — utterly distinct from the shoes of anyone else's mother — when she came to visit.

My own mother and father were there every day, several times a day. For the first two weeks, until I was out of danger, one of them slept in the hospital every night. They were not allowed to touch me. They had to stand several feet back from the bed in their hospital gowns and masks, but they were there every day. And every day before she left, my mother would step forward, lower her mask, and risk death by kissing me.

three

After fifteen days and nights, the fever, the pain, the sweating, and the hallucinations all began gradually to subside—though not yet the screaming of the man down the hall—and I began to come slowly out of the delirium of illness into some normal summer afternoons. I found I could hear clearly the words my mother spoke to me now, as she moved around the room to put flowers in a vase or adjust the curtain at the window, relaying the news of Sookie and Bets and the phone calls from my friend Jim Condill. Once the doctors were certain that my fever was gone for good, a nurse was allowed to open a window, and then I could even feel a breeze come through and ruffle the sheet that was covering me. I could hear the leaves moving on the trees just outside, and I could even hear, every once in a while, the voices of three or four boys playing baseball somewhere outdoors. I was returning to the sweet air and light of ordinary days. The sounds the nurses made now when they entered my room seemed gratifyingly familiar again, and now that the danger had passed they dared to speak to me casually, to say good morning, to talk about the weather.

I found I could still breathe and move my eyes and the few fingers on my left hand. I could not move my head far enough to see these fingers move, but I knew they were moving; I could sense them moving, and if I strained my eyes, I could see a little blur of motion on the periphery of my vision.

It turned out I was not only weak, I was also stiff, as though rigor mortis had set in prematurely. When the nerves die, the inactive muscles shrivel and tighten until they are as taut as piano wires. So I was doubly immobilized, by weakness and by this strange rigidity. But I was alive.

Coming out alive, one would think, is a great victory. I thought it was, and I half-expected some celebrations to be going on, but I couldn't help noticing that the nurses and interns still looked a little grim around the edges, as though survival might be a mixed blessing at best. No one said: You'll be up and around in no time at all.

Still, I was no longer infectious, no longer in danger of dying, and so I was soon ready to be moved down the hall into a room in the children's ward. My mother was there that morning, to walk next to the wheeled cart as I was rolled out of the isolation ward, while the nurses who stayed behind in my old room seized everything in it—flowers, get-well cards, the clothes I had worn to the hospital—and put them in a bag to burn. They stripped my bed, to take sheets and pillowcases and mattress cover to be sterilized.

I was wheeled back down the corridor through which Mrs. Fuller had carried me several weeks before, through the double doors, and into the children's ward, where little kids in wheelchairs, some on crutches, and others—kids who had been there for appendectomies or other of the slings and arrows of early life—had their rooms. I was given my own room, apart from the other children, who were all at least several years younger than I was, and so, even out of the isolation ward, I still lived a life somewhat apart.

But after I was settled in this new room, visitors began immediately to arrive—nurses from the ward, patients from next door, family and friends—eager above all to tell their stories of having been sick, or having had surgery, or their near escapes, or their friends and relatives who had been sick, or stories they had heard of people who had had polio that summer.

Ever since, I have been the recipient of stories from people.

A teenage boy from a Nebraska farm was sent home by his doctor with a diagnosis of the flu. His parents were away on a trip. He spent the next day stacking hay and hoeing cockleburs, using a big stick as a crutch; the next day he got out of bed and fell to the floor. He fell down six times before he got out of the house on his way to his chores, where the neighbors found him lying in the barnyard and encouraged his brother to take him to the hospital.

A seventeen-year-old boy was taken to the hospital in an ambulance. When the drivers loaded him into the back, the doctor told them to cover him with a rubber sheet and, over that, a blanket. When his mother asked why, the doctor said, "Because we don't know if he's contagious, and we don't want to take any chances."

One boy came to the hospital complaining he could hardly walk, but the doctor thought he was faking it, so he made the boy run up and down the hospital corridor to see if he would fall.

One nine-year-old girl was put through a series of muscle tests that seemed inconclusive. She was a child who loved to dance, and so, evidently as part of the diagnosis, someone in the hospital room danced with her around the beds. She said: "That was the last time I ever danced."

One six-year-old boy in the isolation ward said that, for a while, he thought a flock of angels was having a picnic across the room from him.

Some children (not at Sherman, but at other hospitals I heard about) had not been told what they had, because it was thought it might be too great a shock for them. And so they discovered for themselves. One boy, when he had his spine tapped, understood what the test might signify, and he lay anxiously in his hospital room, waiting to find out whether or not he had polio. "The answer was not long in coming. In just a short time, a nurse came to the door of my room and closed it. She did so without saying a word. That is how I learned I had polio."

Another boy acquired from his visitors the biggest collection of comic books he had ever had. When he dropped one, he got out of bed to pick it up, crumpled into a heap, and found he couldn't get up off the floor again.

One kid was resting peacefully in his hospital bed when someone came into the room and pulled a sheet up over his face. He thought nothing of it until later that day one of his wardmates asked him what his name was; when he said his name, the wardmate handed him the afternoon paper containing a list of polio fatalities, and he saw his name on the list.

One boy's uncle had given him a black plastic Hopalong Cassidy bank when the boy was in the isolation ward. When he was moved into the regular children's ward, after his two- or three-week stay in isolation, the nurses threw away the contaminated Hopalong Cassidy bank, along with its savings.

Doctors were mostly irrelevant, and they knew it, except

insofar as they could give some moral support. Some doctors must have been embarrassed by this, or angry, maybe. One doctor came into a boy's room to report the results of the spinal tap, and asked the boy if he knew what infantile paralysis was. The boy said no. "Polio," the doctor said. The boy said he had heard of it, but didn't know what it was really. "Well," said the doctor, "that's what you've got. You've got polio, and you did a good job of it. You're going to be crippled from the top of your shoulders down to your toes."

A boy from Nebraska named Robert Hall had an old family friend for his doctor, a man named Rich Young who was dying himself from Parkinson's disease. And each morning Dr. Young—wealthy enough to retire by that point in his career—would shuffle and lurch his way down the corridor of the isolation ward, leaning far forward, as though into the wind, to make headway with his shaky steps, to visit his patients. He carried a little chrome hammer to test the reflexes of the children in the ward, his hand shaking so much it seemed impossible he could ever hit the mark just below the kneecap, but he always managed to strike home. And after he would test the dead reflexes, he would look Bob Hall in the eye and say, "Bob, are you all right?" And no matter how bad the boy felt—with Dr. Young looking him in the eye, he wouldn't be considering simply the state of his body, he said; he would be making a "total response"—he would rise to the occasion and say yes.

One of the first things anyone brought me after I had been taken out of the isolation ward was a copy of *Life* magazine, in which there appeared a detailed story about the Kinsey Report on sexual practices in America that had just been published. My friends Bob and Jim left the magazine with me, and I struggled, with my few good fingers, to hold it, and—with my neck so stiff, the nurses could put only a thin pillow under my head—to read it. As I read it, I could feel the stirrings of an erection. And so I could check that off the list I hadn't known I was making in my head: My ability to have sex was intact. Not that I'd ever had sex or knew quite what to do with this information at the moment.

(My mother and father found this copy of *Life,* discreetly removed it from the room, ripped out the pages about the Kinsey Report, and put the magazine back on my bedside table.)

The second gift I remember came from my high school English teacher, Maude Strouss—an old maid, as I thought of her then, a woman probably just a year or two shy of re-tirement, with tight curls of hair that had been (badly) dyed coal black. She lived with the high school algebra teacher, Grace Wandke. They were odd women, good teachers, awk-ward in any setting outside the classroom, shy, almost reclu-sive. Miss Strouss gave me a copy of Plato's *Symposium.* It was the first book I ever read, aside from the school assignments I skimmed before I turned to the comic books that I read over and over. Why she imagined I'd be interested, I'll never know.

But as I lay in bed, I had come to understand that what-ever vague plans I may once have had to make my way in the world with my body were now useless. Henceforth, I would have to use my head. And my head was empty. And so I filled it with Plato. In fact, I devoured the *Symposium,* and asked Miss Strouss to bring me more. She brought me *Crito, Phaedo,* and the *Apology,* and more, and then more. Before I could hold a book with all my fingers, I had read all of Plato. I loved the dialogue form, the opposing arguments, the turmoil of conflicting ideas and feelings; he spoke to my own warring mind and heart.

Only years later did I think back and realize that what Miss Strouss had first brought me, Plato's book about love, was her extraordinary way—this idiosyncratic, introverted woman of mysterious erotic preferences—of telling me she loved me. Her gift has informed my entire life.

My father, commuting every day to Chicago, came to the hospital nearly every day after work for the evening visiting hours and always on weekends.

Bets came less often. It was thought that young people were too endangered by visits to the hospital.

My friend Jim needed special permission to visit.

Stevie never came to visit. She was, after all, a young girl, only thirteen; it was hard for her to know just what to do.

My mother was there every day, to see that I was comfortable, to fix my sheets, bring me cookies or brownies or fresh fruit, tell me the news from home, the news of my friends, to read to me, to ask the nurses for one favor or another for me. My mother asked the doctors whether muscles might be taken from her and transplanted to my body. She asked them the first time almost immediately after I entered the hospital, and then she went on asking persistently for years afterward, always ready to hope some new medical advance had been made. Her question made me cringe; I wanted her to give it up. I myself felt I needed to get on with my life, harboring no false hopes. And yet, of course, I loved her for it. She was the one, in my world at that time, who never gave up.

In the children's ward, at lunchtime, one of the frustrated patients would dip the cover of his straw into his butter and blow the paper cover up to stick on the ceiling. Another would follow suit, and another, until the ceilings of the rooms were festooned with hundreds of rancid straw covers.

One boy perfected a technique for getting his wheelchair up to high speed and then flipping it forward just in front of the nurses' station, sending him belly flopping to the floor so that the pretty young nurses would rush over and pick him up and fawn over him.

Another boy had an arm and a leg in a cast—I don't remember what he had done; he hadn't had polio. He could get his wheelchair up to amazing speeds, moving his arm back and forth from one wheel to another to propel the chair down a corridor and then grab one wheel and spin on down the hall—a practice the nurses put a stop to after he ran into a cart full of medicines one day and sent the glass containers flying to the walls.

I heard of one kid who got some sticky stuff from the nurses' station and glued together another kid's paralyzed toes.

But usually the kids worked together. One who could move his arms would team up with another who could move his legs, or one who had strong enough lungs to shout would call for a nurse, while others built a trap. In one room full of boys, a couple of them got hold of a four-inch-long aluminum tube, which they plugged at one end with a bottle cap and secured to a block of wood. When they put match heads and cigarette lighter fluid down into the tube and then lit it with a match, it became a cannon that spewed out a gush of fire.

But the nurses were not defenseless victims; early in the morning, when it was time to wake us up, some nurses could throw a cold, wet washcloth all the way from outside the door, across a room, and hit an adolescent boy square in the face.

Two nurses' aides cared for me in the children's ward — the blond Barbara, sweet and plump, devoted and caring; and the dark-haired, bespectacled Adele, slender and lovely and sexy. Both were just a couple of years older than I was. I think Barbara was in love with me. I was in love with Adele. She was not in love with me. One day, some weeks after I had gotten out of the isolation ward and was able to hold a camera in one hand, I asked her if I could take a picture of her. She turned sideways, putting into sudden silhouette the beautiful contours of her breasts, her stomach, her buttocks, the small of her back. She put one hand up to hold the hair back from her face, and she threw back her head and laughed with pure delight. I still have the picture. I look at it, and the feeling of that moment comes back vividly: deep, deep longing.

In the book she wrote about her polio, *Small Steps*, Peg Kehret told of a girl named Alice who shared her room in the Sheltering Arms Hospital in Minneapolis. Alice, who was thirteen years old, had been in the hospital for ten years when Peg arrived. In fact, after Alice had been in the hospital for only a few months, the doctors had said she was well enough to go home, but, because she was badly disabled, her parents didn't want her, and so the hospital had become her permanent home. When Peg's parents came to visit, they asked Peg and Alice and the other roommates what treats they wished for on the next visit. And the other girls asked for licorice or marshmallows or a comic book. But Alice asked for nothing. "At first," Peg wrote, "I thought she was being ornery; then I realized Alice had been at the Sheltering Arms for so long she didn't remember things like comic books and marshmallows. Licorice and potato chips were beyond her realm of experience. She didn't know what to ask for because she did not know what she was missing."

Was this fair? Somehow, we had blown by the idea of fairness so quickly, had left it so far back in the distance, that I sometimes marvel I still retain any concept of it at all. Fairness must be an amazingly powerful, sturdy human need to have withstood such a battering. Who could have held on to it in the face of everything I saw in the hospital? And yet somewhere, deep down, the unfairness of it all must have gnawed at me constantly. Somewhere, deep down, there must have been an insistent, irritating, nattering little voice saying over and over, Is this fair? And another little voice saying, Will you just get over it?

Some children who had had polio passed through the hospital in a few days, or a month, or two. When it came time for them to pack up their hospital game books and get-well cards and flowers and go home, the rest of us looked on with envy mixed with the good will we felt for those who had become our friends: these lucky kids, for whom polio had hardly been more than a bad case of flu, a summer adventure, a near escape to talk about to their classmates. With each departure, those who stayed behind felt they had taken one more step backward, had lost yet one more piece of ground, had retreated that much further from the prospect of recovery. In the field of neurology, there is a nearly tautological saying that the doctors repeat like a mantra: If you are improving, you will improve. The more slowly you improve, the less likely, every day, becomes the prospect of a full recovery. With each child who left the hospital, the slowness with which the rest of us were recovering became more and more apparent. No one told us how we were doing, or how we would do; how long it would take for us to recover, or how much we might recover; whether we would be able to get out of our beds, whether we would walk again or not: this was something we discovered for ourselves, gradually, as the days went by and we saw who improved quickly and who didn't, who went home and who stayed behind. Imperceptibly, the simple terror of the first moments in the hospital was replaced by a chaos of emotions, of new denial, anxiety, determination to prove everyone wrong. Of the eight or ten kids who passed through the polio unit at Sherman Hospital that year, by the end of the summer I would be the only one still there.

Of those who were struck by polio in those days, in all its forms, from mildest to most severe, most recovered with very little or no damage. No one has reliable statistics on these matters. A very small number, perhaps 1.5 percent, died from polio. The rest were left with a bizarre, unquantifiable array of crippling effects and prospects for recovery in whole or in part.

There was a television set in a common room on the children's floor, where the kids would gather in wheelchairs and on wheeled pallets. This was the Golden Age of television: the Sid Caesar comedy hour, wrestling, Howdy Doody, weather reports, and test patterns that would occupy the screen for hours at a time. Occasionally, we would watch the story of someone who had fallen ill and recovered—and although we were only children, we knew we were being had. No one's experience of being seriously sick has ever been shown truly on television. No one's. Not once. I don't know why. I suppose television writers have been ill, one or two of them, and maybe the odd television director has been sick, and perhaps a television producer has known someone who has had some disease or other. But the plot on television is always the same: Someone is struck by something; there is suffering; it is immensely sad; the stricken person is sad; the audience is made to empathize, pity, and cry; and then—very soon, before the burden of illness becomes too difficult—there is the full recovery, the happy, vigorous return to life itself, reaffirmation, optimism, victory. No child I knew at Sherman believed it.

Of course, none of the kids, no matter how young, could bear all the tear-jerking in these stories, which they knew was manipulative and contemptible. You might think that was because they had repressed their own sadness, but that was not the case. Those who had been seriously damaged by polio or by some disorder from birth, some problem with a heart valve, or some other serious childhood disease, felt their sadness; they cried from time to time in the privacy of their own rooms. More than that, they felt, as I did, a torrent of emotions, of fear and loneliness, panic and despair, hostility and cynicism, hope, recurring hope, a crazy rage, hope returning once again when it had been forgotten, the inadequacy of being small, the anxiety that comes of being kept in ignorance by doctors, the wish to be naughty, the growing suspicion that the doctors didn't know anything anyway, the cavalier toughness of a war hero in a Hollywood movie, John Wayne's disdain for self-pity, the memory of almost dancing, the thought of escape, of flying out the window of the hospital, of sudden miraculous recovery, hopelessness, relentless boredom, unreasoning optimism, a desire to be touched if only inadvertently by a nurse, hatred for the sunshine coming through the window, longing for a visit from my mother. I felt, the other children felt, such a chaos of emotions that the weak treacle of sorrow on television seemed completely unbelievable.

Then, too, I think it is intact people who like to experience the feelings of sorrow and loss and bitterness over and over again—and who always ask injured people about these feelings, to conjure them up and experience them vicariously. Intact people like to see stories about people who lose something, are filled with deep sorrow, and recover—and to see these stories over and over and over—I suppose because they are afraid for their own bodies and seek constant reassurance. But once your body is broken, you no longer need those reassurances, or, maybe, no longer find them so reassuring. And meanwhile, so many other feelings come to vie for attention—new, previously unimagined emotions, of astonishment, for example, at the condition we found ourselves in, of wonder at how suddenly and completely our lives could change; of immense awe at the power of nature to turn on us and knock us right out of the park.

For those of us who were not showing some marked recovery right away in the first few weeks, polio would not be like pneumonia or a broken leg, where, after several months, the difficulty disappears. No one recovers from a serious onslaught of polio—just as no one recovers from diabetes or multiple sclerosis or schizophrenia or AIDS or so many other illnesses. Some people recover partly, or for a while, sometimes even for a long while; they are given a reprieve, allowed to resume a nearly "normal" life, with some residual damage that is more or less vexing. The damage that has been done is incorporated into their life; if it is something more than minor, it alters their life, is knit in to everything they do, shapes their careers and marriages and partnerships and relationships with their children. They come back from the original onslaught, and then, some years later, discover they must recover again, and then yet again—until recovery really is out of the question; they come to the end of their life recognizing that damage is finally inescapable in life. If they live long enough, everyone comes to know that there are no simple, made-for-television triumphs in life, no way of isolating trials and recoveries from the rest of their life, setting off sickness in a separate compartment, getting over it and going on. Their final coming to terms, their triumph, if it comes, always takes longer, is far more complicated, and is far more profound.

And meanwhile, if they become writers, they begin to notice that even the way they form a sentence and tell a story is affected by who they have become. I find, when I write, that I really don't want to write well-made sentences and paragraphs, narratives that flow, structures that have a sense of wholeness and balance, books that feel intact. Intact people should write intact books with sound narratives built of sound paragraphs that unfold with a sense of dependable cause and effect, solid structures you can rely on. That is not my experience of the world. I like a book that feels like a crystal goblet that has been thrown to the floor and shattered, so that its pieces, when they are picked up and arranged on a table, still describe a whole glass, but the glass itself lies in shards. To me, sentences should veer and smash up, careen out of control; get under way and find themselves unable to stop, switch directions suddenly and irrevocably, break off, come to a sighing inconclusiveness. If a writer's writings constitute a "body of work," then my body of work, to feel true to me, must feel fragmented. And then, too, if you find it hard to walk down the sidewalk, you like, in the freedom of your mind, to make a sentence that leaps and dances now and then before it comes to a sudden stop.

four

These are things people will tell you in the hospital — not your parents, but other visitors and, often, the nurses — things they know, or hear from others, or pick up from books or newspapers, things that are true and things that are false and things that are both true and false and bizarre and pointless or no longer relevant all at the same time and stuff you didn't want to hear anyway because who cares but you can't get away from being given the information because you are a captive audience, such as:

orange juice can cause polio;

contaminated milk can cause polio;

some children were no longer allowed out in their own yards;

Minneapolis forbade all children under the age of fifteen from going to movies, churches, and amusement parks;

cold water was dangerous, because FDR got polio after swimming in the cold water near his summer home;

one mother made her children wear white cotton gloves when they went to the movies;

some mothers attached little pouches containing a piece of alum to their children's underwear;

people said you could tell if you were getting polio because your neck got stiff, so a lot of mothers gave their children periodic "polio tests," having their children sit up straight in a chair and touch their chins to their chests;

the Masons canceled their picnics;

a synagogue canceled its ice cream social;

people said that truck farmers were using sewage water to irrigate crops outside Denver, and there had been outbreaks of polio in Florida and Arkansas after they got some truck-garden vegetables from the Denver area, so people needed to scrub their fruit and vegetables really well;

some people switched to canned fruit, or ate no fruit at all;

a Dr. Armstrong, thinking you could keep people from getting polio by coating the olfactory nerves, sprayed picric acid and alum up the noses of 4,600 people in Alabama;

one family, hearing that travel was especially dangerous for young children, left their seven-year-old child at home alone when they took the other kids on vacation;

people said you might have a predisposition to polio if you had sinus trouble; a Dr. Schultz, thinking zinc sulfate might block the olfactory lobes, sprayed that up the noses of 5,000 kids in Toronto;

some mothers boiled their dishes;

some people wiped all surfaces with alcohol;

the incidence of polio could be correlated with levels of nuclear radiation, which could be calculated by the annual volume of bean production in the Midwest;

one person didn't know she had polio until she couldn't pick up some utensils out of a kitchen drawer; two weeks later, when her husband complained to the doctor of a headache, he was told it was psychosomatic, and then he collapsed, spent a year and a half in the hospital, and came out unable to move his arms or legs, and his wife was dead;

polio went through a family of seven that summer, showing up as nothing but headaches and sore throats and diarrhea, which they thought nothing of until their seven-year-old caught it and died;

at the D. T. Watson Home for Crippled Children in Pittsburgh, two teenage boys, former high school football stars who had come down with polio, committed suicide;

a man in an iron lung got married;

a three-year-old boy whose arm was paralyzed was seen showing his friends how he could pick up marbles with his toes;

another boy who had had polio learned to chew his food by moving his jaw with his hand;

polio could be cured with "the juice of the gourd;"

polio could be cured by eating "slightly radioactive" breakfast cereal;

a fifteen-year-old girl in an iron lung read books using a machine that projected the pages on a ceiling; she used her mouth to turn the pages; she had learned to write with her toes, and had mastered algebra all by herself;

one boy had learned to turn the pages of his book by using a stick in his mouth;

a woman in an iron lung had her books rigged up on an overhead rack; the pages had to be turned by a nurse, so the woman had had three books at a time set up for her so that she could read six pages before needing a turning; she said she always tried to choose three very different sorts of books so that she wouldn't get them mixed up in her mind;

a man learned to write, and to type, with his feet, and decided to go into philosophy as his profession—because it was something he could do in his head. His father celebrated the decision by giving him a beer label advertising "Hemlock";

at the military hospital in Benghazi, in North Africa, there were no iron lungs, so the Royal Electrical and Mechanical Engineers made one out of a coffin;

the radio program "Inner Sanctum" ran an episode in which a man got into an iron lung to demonstrate how it worked, and his wife and her lover locked him in, turned up the pressure, and killed him;

lots of people with bulbar polio needed to have a tracheotomy, an incision just below the Adam's apple, to have a tube inserted to supply them with oxygen, and to drain away the mucus so they wouldn't suffocate in their own saliva;

no one ever knew which muscles might be attacked by the polio virus — sometimes one leg, sometimes two, sometimes an arm and leg, sometimes the brain. You never knew. It could take out two brothers at the same time, and the muscles it affected would be entirely different in each of them. And, after you had it, and you started doing physical therapy, you never knew which muscles would recover or how much they would recover;

there was a new surgical technique for treating polio, called neurotripsy, in which the nerves were crushed so that new nerves would be stimulated to grow;

another surgical technique called for the "bands of diseased tissue" to be sliced out of the muscles, or tendons woven in around the muscle tissue;

some people were killed by iron lungs, because the muscles they still had would try to help them breathe in a rhythm different from the rhythm of the iron lung, and they would fight the iron lung until they died of exhaustion.

Someone once said: We are all veterans, only of different wars.

five

The background:

There is an Egyptian stele, or stone carving, from some-where between 1580 and 1350 B.C. that shows a young man with a drop foot. That foot, hanging down limply as the young man takes a step, the atrophied muscles in his leg too weak to lift his toes, is the telltale polio foot — the earliest recorded evidence of a case of polio.

However, according to Edmund Sass, who got polio that same summer I did, "It was not until the late 1700s . . . that the existence of polio was described with any degree of certainty," and not until 1840 that a German physician named Jacob Heine published a monograph saying that the symptoms of polio suggested some involvement of the spinal cord.

There are, in fact, two principle sorts of polio: spinal and bulbar. In spinal polio — the kind I had — the virus affects the motor neurons of the spinal cord, taking out control of arms and legs, but leaving the sensory cells intact so that all the messages of pain and pleasure, hot and cold, touch and position and balance are still as clear as ever.

(The penis is okay. It works on blood flow, not muscles. People always try to find a tactful way to ask me about this.)

In bulbar polio, the virus may go for the brain, though

more commonly it assaults the motor nerves of the eyes and face and the pharynx and larynx and soft palate, which makes swallowing and speaking and breathing difficult or impossible.

Still, the submicroscopic nature of the polio virus, as Sass says, kept physicians from understanding the nature of the disease for many years. And even though there were ample cases of polio to study in the large outbreaks of the disease in the late nineteenth century, physicians thought the symptoms they were seeing might be caused by teething or upset stomachs.

In the nineteenth century, doctors prescribed bleeding for acute polio patients (as, indeed, for many patients with all sorts of illnesses). The more advanced physicians applied ice to the spines of polio patients or rubbed mercury ointment on them to stimulate blisters, for some reason. One doctor advised putting a red-hot iron over the affected area to cauterize the bad stuff. Another recommended amputating paralyzed limbs. Early in the twentieth century, polio patients were zapped with electrical currents on the theory that this would jolt the muscles back into action.

For some reason, and no one knows why, polio changed in the early twentieth century from an endemic disease, ever present at a low and usually unnoticed level in the general population, to an epidemic disease, in which flare-ups caused acute illness, paralysis, and death.

Just how polio is transmitted and caught was not known. Indeed, it is not entirely understood even now. The best evidence suggests that the virus is excreted in the stool and passed along by hand-to-hand contact — or maybe by using a restroom in a diner along the highway from Illinois to Colorado. No one knows.

It is thought that many children used to catch polio as

toddlers through contact with open sewers and privies. At that early age, they were still protected by maternal antibodies, so they had mild, nonparalytic cases and developed their own antibodies to protect them from later exposure. Then, as sewage systems improved in the developed countries in the early twentieth century, kids were no longer exposed to the virus in early childhood, and so took the full onslaught in their teens. Having developed no antibodies, some were paralyzed. Thus, as Jane S. Smith has written in her history of polio, many people believe that "paralytic polio was an inadvertent by-product of modern sanitary conditions," a sign of national progress, first occurring in epidemic proportions among the more privileged classes in the industrialized countries of the West.

Polio's suddenness and unpredictability—the unknowability of where it came from, when and where it might strike, and how severely—gave it the mystique and fearsomeness almost of the bubonic plague as it swept through the country, even though it was never the leading killer in the world. Nor did the polio virus usually result in paralysis. Most people experienced only mild flulike symptoms. The virus entered the central nervous system in just a small minority of cases. How it reached the central nervous system remains unknown.

Muscle fatigue and strain appear to be predisposing factors to paralysis. No one knows why.

Recently, it has been seen that patients in the "Third World" suffering from polio, if given injections of antibiotics or antimalarials, will develop paralysis within a week. No one knows how this mechanism works.

Pregnancy, tonsillectomy, and other medical procedures for the nose and throat predispose one toward polio. No one knows why.

The disease occurred 35 times more often in August than in April. No one knows why.

The best hypothesis about the dramatic increase of epidemic polio in the twentieth century is the improvement in sewage systems, but during the epidemic years, the incidence of polio varied greatly from year to year and region to region — unrelated to sewage system improvements or any other identifiable factor.

The reason for the random appearance of polio, the manner of its transmission, the reason it paralyzed some people and not others remain a mystery. Now that polio is nearly gone from the world, and there is not enough of the disease anymore to be studied, these mysteries will probably never be solved.

In 1916, there was a large outbreak of polio in the United States; New York City, the hardest-hit spot in the country, had nine thousand cases. Well-to-do families fled from the city to the surrounding countryside. The citizens of Pennsylvania and New Jersey and Connecticut, frightened by the influx of New Yorkers, persuaded their public officials to impose quarantines. In Pennsylvania, medical inspectors were sent out to guard the roads coming into the state. In Paterson, New Jersey, officials announced that no "nonresidents" would be allowed to stay in that town. In Setauket, Long Island, residents posted a sign: "Warning. — We are informed that families from the infected parts of New York City and Brooklyn are offering high prices for rooms and houses here. While we sympathize fully with all who are suffering from this dread disease . . . we certainly should be very careful to whom we extend the hospitality of our village . . ." It was soon clear that such measures were not at all effective in stopping polio, but nonetheless, for the next several decades, civil authorities all across the country tried to control the spread of the disease with isolation and quarantine.

In the 1920s, the medical community was momentarily excited by the prospect of a "cure" for polio. Researchers had developed a "convalescent serum" manufactured from the blood of monkeys and humans who had recently recovered from polio. Some serum came from horses. The serum was injected into people who had had polio. None of it was effective.

In the 1920s, too, the first iron lung appeared, made of a cylindrical sheet-metal tank with vacuum cleaner hoses attached to it. It was said that the earliest iron lungs could be heard from a half-mile away. The machine was invented by Philip Drinker, a young assistant professor in the Department of Ventilation and Illumination of the Harvard School of Public Health, who had previously spent his career with machines that made and measured dust. The principle of the machine, as Drinker said, was simple: to create alternately positive and negative air pressure to make the diaphragm of the person inside the machine expand and contract. The optimal diameter for the hole through which the patient's head was put was based on information from the Knox Hat Company, and the appropriate diameter for the rubber collar that sealed in the air pressure around the patient's neck was based on information from the Cluett Peabody shirt company. The idea for portholes, through which doctors and nurses could minister to the patient, came from a chance visit to a boat dock.

At roughly this same time, too, it was commonly thought that immobilizing the limbs would somehow be beneficial, and so patients who were not in iron lungs were usually put into plaster casts — legs straight, arms outstretched, like Leonardo's perfectly proportioned man. Some were strung up in traction; others were put in splints. One boy, who later became a doctor himself, was put in the so-called Toronto splints, leather-covered things that held his knees bent, his legs spread apart, suspended motionless for nine months. In this way, muscles were allowed to become completely useless — stiff and painful beyond imagining, and wasted away from lack of exercise or movement of any kind.

In 1921, luckily for the rest of us, Franklin Delano Roosevelt — thirty-nine years old, a nominee for vice president of the United States the year before — contracted polio, and no polio patient after that was treated quite as badly as the standard practice had previously dictated. The stigma of the disease did not disappear; it has not disappeared even yet. But with Roosevelt, it eased up. Before Roosevelt's day, according to the historian Paul K. Longmore, people with physical handicaps were usually "kept at home, out of sight, in back bedrooms by families who felt a mixture of embarassment and shame about their presence." Disabled children were barred from attending public school. According to an influential orthopedic text of 1911, "A failure in the moral training of a cripple means the evolution of an individual detestable in character, a menace and a burden to the community, who is only apt to graduate into the mendicant and criminal classes."

Roosevelt tried everything to overcome his disability. He heard that the waters of Warm Springs, Georgia, would "cure" polio, and so he tried those waters in 1924. Of course, the waters cured nothing, but they felt good — and the sense that one was *doing* something was irresistible. Roosevelt purchased the dilapidated health resort he visited in Warm Springs, renovated it, turned it into his second home, and opened it to others who had had polio and other physical disabilities.

In 1926, Roosevelt started the Warm Springs Foundation, to generate support for the work being done there. The foundation was run by Basil O'Connor, who had been Roosevelt's law partner, and O'Connor hired an insurance salesman named Keith Morgan to help with fund-raising. When Roosevelt was elected president in 1932, Morgan had the idea of staging a national Birthday Ball for the president, a series of parties across the country that would raise money for Warm Springs. By November of 1933, no less than six thousand charitable balls had been organized around the country, and so much money was brought in on the president's birthday on January 30 that by 1937, the foundation had been reorganized as the National Foundation for Infantile Paralysis, dedicated to raising money to help those who had had polio and to help pay their hospital and therapy bills. After the first of the Birthday Balls, Paul de Kruif, who in 1926 had published a best-selling book called *Microbe Hunters,* said to one of the Warm Springs people, "Why do you use all that dough to dip cripples in warm water? That doesn't cure them any more than it cured you or the President. Why don't you ask the President to devote a part of that big dough to research on polio *prevention?* Nobody knows a thing about that." De Kruif's remark made its way to Roosevelt, and thenceforth, some of the foundation's money was earmarked to underwrite research for an effective vaccine against polio.

One of the earliest foundation-supported attempts to develop a vaccine was conducted by Maurice Brodie, who developed a concoction by grinding up spinal cords of monkeys infected by the polio virus. He tried to deactivate the virus by exposing it to formalin (a formaldehyde mixture), and in 1935 he tried it out on twenty monkeys and three thousand children. Just what happened is not clear, but, as John R. Paul has written in his history of polio, "something went wrong and Brodie's vaccine was never used again."

Meanwhile, John Kolmer began his work with a live polio virus taken from monkeys. He weakened (or attenuated) the virus by mixing it with a number of chemicals and refrigerating it for two weeks. John R. Paul refers to the work of Brodie and Kolmer as "kitchen chemistry," and declared Kolmer's vaccine a "veritable witches' brew." John Rowan Wilson, in his history of the search for a polio vaccine, said that Kolmer's method of production of the vaccine was "hair-raisingly amateurish, the therapeutic equivalent of bath-tub gin." Kolmer "indulged in 'the usual preliminary heroics'," Tony Gould wrote in his history of polio, "of trying out his vaccine on himself," and then on his wife, his children, a few monkeys and twenty-two others, and then, unfortunately, he sent out batches in 1935 to physicians to inoculate twelve thousand children. The vaccine did not work. Indeed, it caused a number of cases of polio, some of them fatal.

So disastrous were the vaccine trials of Brodie and Kolmer that no such trials were attempted again for twenty years.

six

By 1938, the year I was born, the fund-raising campaign of the National Foundation for Infantile Paralysis was in full cry. O'Connor and Morgan had augmented the foundation's annual campaign, which took place every January, to include a radio address by President Roosevelt and a luncheon with Mrs. Roosevelt at the White House. And they had persuaded some Hollywood studio executives (always anxious about antitrust legislation) to provide a few dozen stars for the president's annual Birthday Ball: "to dance, so that others may walk."

One of the Hollywood celebrities who became enthusiastic enough about the charitable event to attend a planning meeting in Los Angeles, the comedian Eddie Cantor, came up with the idea of giving the annual fund-raising event a catchy name. Playing on the title of the popular newsreel "The March of Time" that was regularly screened in movie theaters around the country in those days, Cantor suggested that the foundation's annual January campaign be called "The March of Dimes," and that everyone across America be urged to send a dime directly to the White House to fight polio. The week of the January 1938 Birthday Ball, the Lone Ranger asked all the boys and girls listening to his radio show to send their dimes to the president, and a few days later, the usual volume of letters to the White House jumped from 5,000 a day to 30,000, and the next day to 50,000, and the following day to 150,000 — "scrawled and finger-marked envelopes," as the White House chief of mails said, "from every kid who could get his hands on a dime" — $268,000 in dimes.

Henceforth, philanthropy and showbiz were inseparable in the fight against polio. Jack Benny, who was famous for jokes about his stinginess, incorporated a running gag into his radio show about what a hard time the campaign had in prying a dime out of him to send to the president. Kate Smith sang for the March of Dimes. Jascha Heifetz played his violin. Humphrey Bogart and Jimmy Cagney went on the radio impersonating "tough guy" dimes to advertise the fight against polio. Judy Garland and Mickey Rooney made a short to be shown in movie houses. So did Jimmy Stewart. "Voices quavered," as Jane S. Smith has written, "eyes watered, and the audience was told how, right now, each of them should reach into purse or pocket and get out some money. Then the lights would come on and the ushers would pass up and down the aisles with collection baskets."

After December 7, 1941, when the Japanese bombed Pearl Harbor, the United States entered World War II, and the country became preoccupied with the war, contributions to the March of Dimes did not decline, as everyone thought they would, but rather rose.

"Not until we have removed the shadow of the Crippler from the future of every child," President Roosevelt wrote in an open letter to the country, "can we furl the flags of battle and still the trumpets of attack. The fight against infantile paralysis is a fight to the finish, and the terms are unconditional surrender."

When the movie ushers went to war, the collection boxes were handed over to members of ladies' clubs around the country. America's Sweetheart, Mary Pickford, was made honorary director of the women volunteers. Soon, women were going door to door for the March of Dimes. In Phoenix, according to Kathryn Black's *In the Shadow of Polio,* the Mothers' March on Polio in 1950 asked people to leave their porch lights on as a signal that they had a contribution waiting for the volunteers (so that all the skinflints who left their lights off would be publicly humiliated). "A gift of a penny from a family who can only place a candle in a bottle on their porch will be as welcome as a hundred dollars from a home with an elaborate porch light." And then kids in Arizona went from house to house, knocking on doors in Morse code for SOS (three short taps, three long, and three short again) to let folks know they were there for a contribution. A former polio patient walked across the state of Idaho to collect pledges. Society women collected money on street corners.

The National Foundation's Radio and Film Department turned out heartbreaking stories to be shown at fund-raising banquets. The lights would dim, the flickering images or still photographs would come on the screen: the child stricken with polio, the frightened parents rushing the child to the hospital, the child lying pale and emaciated in bed, near death. And then the lights would go up—and that very same child would be there in the banquet hall, making his triumphant way to the microphone, supported by a pair of crutches paid for by the March of Dimes.

Bing Crosby and Danny Kaye were photographed with one little poster boy who, like all poster boys, wore shorts so that the braces on both legs would show. His hair was neatly combed, and he was dressed in a little white shirt with an open collar, and he had been propped up to sit on a table between the two stars. All three of them were smiling—the little boy a little less confidently than the two stars, as though he might be thinking he might topple over onto the floor at any moment.

One of the most popular films, according to Jane Smith, was *The Daily Battle,* "which opened with a dark cloud spreading over playground and farm, mansion and tenement, a cloud that takes the shape of a hunched and sinister figure who cackles over his many victims. The fearful shadow of the Crippler is finally dispelled by a National Foundation volunteer, played by a very young actress later known as Nancy Reagan."

I grew up in this world of March of Dimes hype, but I hardly paid attention to it. It had nothing to do with me. I certainly never thought the Crippler was going to get anyone I knew. According to the stories and the posters themselves, polio was invariably something that happened to kids in other towns.

The foundation's publicity department planted stories in magazines such as *Reader's Digest* about scientific breakthroughs—from research financed by "your dollars." The *New York Times* Sunday magazine ran an article titled "Hope and Courage—That Is Warm Springs," in which the reporter found many wonderful stories. "Take the case of a concert pianist whose hands were spared but whose feet were so affected that it was impossible for him to use the pedals of the piano. He has turned painter and his watercolors are bright and beautiful. That is the spirit of Warm Springs.

"Then there is the girl whom a doctor saw learning how to walk. 'What is her muscle set-up?' he asked.

" 'Muscles? She hasn't any,' he was told. 'She walks with her head!'

"And that is the spirit of Warm Springs."

Another article in the *Times* told of a girl stricken with polio in 1944. At the time of the article, five years later, "she is completely recovered, as is the case with more than 50 per cent of those stricken, thanks to progress in research, diagnosis and care, all heavily financed by the Foundation. Her illness 'is like a bad dream,' says her mother . . . 'now that her father and I watch her playing and walking as easily as any of her friends.' "

Bob Hope, Cary Grant, and Barbara Stanwyck appealed for funds.

In Yakima, Washington, a pancake-eating contest was held: all the flapjacks you could eat for a buck, proceeds to the March of Dimes. The town of Arlington, Virginia, turned over all the dimes its parking meters took in during the month of January. In Colorado, a bowling league raised $11.55 by assessing its members each time they failed to make a strike or a spare.

At one fund-raiser, Eddie Cantor took off his shirt and put it up for auction.

One poster showed a little boy in shorts with suspenders and a white T-shirt, two steel braces on his legs, with the legend "Please! Join the March of Dimes." Another showed a boy before and after: with his head lolling in a neck brace, and then striding out robustly, with the legend "Your dimes did this for me!" Another showed a little girl in a sweet little dress, her hair in Shirley Temple curls, stepping out of a wheelchair;

the legend read, "Look! I can walk again." Another little girl in another sweet little dress, her feet in black patent leather shoes, braces on both legs, crutches on both hands, "I'm winning because of you." A little girl in a white dress, a white bow in her hair, her gaze lifted up to heaven, two crutches, two braces, "Fight Polio!" A little boy in blue jeans, a cowboy shirt, a cowboy hat, six-shooters in holsters at his hips, two crutches — superimposed on a photograph of an American soldier in the trenches with his hand outstretched toward us: "This fight is *yours.*"

This was a fight anyone could join. Maybe the war against Hitler had to be left to the soldiers, but every man, woman, and child on the home front could wage the war against polio; it mobilized the entire country. The polio campaign got all mixed up with World War II and being a good American and believing in democracy and pitching in and winning.

In 1938, when Basil O'Connor became the president of the National Foundation for Infantile Paralysis, the federal government was only very marginally engaged in any sort of medical research. The National Institute of Health (later to grow into the "Institutes") sponsored no work outside its own laboratories. The Communicable Diseases Center (now the Centers for Disease Control) was a little operation mostly taken up with keeping track of any outbreaks of malaria that might endanger military bases in the South. By the time I got polio, however, the nongovernmental National Foundation for Infantile Paralysis had 3,000 local chapters, 90,000 year-round volunteers, 2 million part-time volunteers. Only the American Red Cross took in more dollars. The March of Dimes pulled in a vast group of ordinary people, who couldn't afford to attend benefits and dinner dances or endow medical research centers but who wanted, nonetheless, to do something to help the world. The March of Dimes was the first charitable organization to give them that chance, the first organization to say that dimes, and not just dollars, helped.

In the year I got polio, the March of Dimes raised $54 million to finance research and to pay doctors and hospitals and rehabilitation therapists and buy crutches and braces and iron lungs for 74,000 people. The cost for a patient who was in an iron lung could run to $15,000 a year—this at a time when a house could cost less than $10,000. In those days, few people had medical insurance; hardly anyone had insurance that covered the sort of long-term, intensive care that polio patients required. The March of Dimes raised enough money every year to pay the expenses of any polio patient who needed help.

By this time, according to Kathryn Black, whose own mother had polio in 1954, "no plea for contributions was too maudlin. A dummy made of a diving suit, sitting in a wheelchair and wrapped with cloth, was stuck with safety pins. Passers-by were asked to make a contribution and pull out a pin, to 'Help get "Polio Joe" out of pain' . . . To kick off the 1955 fund drive, Richard Nixon, then the vice-president, wiped windshields at a service station, after pulling up in a chauffeur-driven Cadillac."

And by the late summer of 1954, *Time* magazine was reporting that some communities were afraid that polio was sucking up all the money that might otherwise go for other worthy causes. Prefiguring the remarks that would be made several decades later about the fund-raising to combat AIDS, the editorial page in a local Syracuse newspaper complained that "far more money is raised for polio than cancer, heart disease or TB—which have higher death rates." The National

Foundation for Infantile Paralysis, the editorial writer complained, was "greedy and extravagant."

Although I grew up inattentive to it all, this was the culture—of the March of Dimes, of Polio Joe and Eddie Cantor, and Richard Nixon wiping windshields—that was poised to take me in.

seven

As I lay in bed the first few days out of the isolation ward, getting used to the idea that I hadn't died and taking stock of my body parts, I found that I could move the fingers of my left hand over and over and over again—to begin, on my own, some exercises to regain my strength, and I worked at that obsessively. I had begun, too, to be able to flex my wrist just a little, to start to build back the muscles of my forearm. But still, my entire body—like the body of everyone else just out of the polio isolation ward—was so stiffened that it approximated the condition of a body left in a peat bog for several centuries.

The first part of rehabilitation for one who has had polio is to bring warmth to the muscles in order to relax them, to let them move, and to start to stretch them out again, and, finally, to discover which, if any, muscles have been spared and to rebuild the strength of those muscles with exercise. The warmth came, starting four or five days after I was out of isolation, by wrapping my body in Army surplus khaki wool blankets soaked in hot water, and then wrapping plastic sheeting over the blankets. This was the famous Sister Kenny treatment technique. It was such a bizarre, disgusting procedure that no one who had polio in those days has forgotten what seemed like a punishment for having gotten sick. The blankets itched, of course, and were either so hot to begin with that they scorched and burned — mere warmth was never considered sufficient — or else they got cold and clammy in short order. Many people who had polio back then are still unable to wear wool clothing of any kind, and certainly not during a rain, when the smell of the wet wool possesses almost hallucinogenic powers.

Here, finally, occurred the moment of despair. Lying stiff, immobile, barely able to breathe under the thick layers of wet wool, chest weighted down by the heavy blankets; with nothing to do but endure the hour or two or three of searing heat and useless cold: this was the moment that tears came at last to my eyes. This was the moment I thought this process of recovery was going to fail, that it was much too slow, that I never would be better, that I was forever — that dreaded word — crippled, that all my strategies for denial and fighting back and outsmarting all my feelings by some heroic act of understanding were pathetic and worthless; that I might as well quit, give up, sink down, be taken care of; that I was, without recourse, a ruined child. This was the moment of deepest anguish, and it was not one moment alone, but a moment that recurred again and again day after day as, for the next two weeks, the nurses would bring in the steaming wool blankets and engulf me, take away even the little bit of movement I was capable of in my fingers; then the tears would come again, the tears and desolation, the hatred of my own body, the feeling of shame at what I had become, the shame of wanting to give up, the shame of feeling sorry for myself, the shame of how I was now the child of whom my parents' friends would say, "Oh, I'm sorry, I'm so sorry," the boy who would never be his father's pride, the boy who would be pitied. Then tears came and came, and sorrow submerged me entirely.

And when the nurses would finally come back to remove the last of the wet wool blankets and replace them with new, dry sheets, and leave me alone to turn my head as best I could to look out the window at the sky, then I was quiet for long, long hours on into the darkness and the night. And the sense of despair eased into grief and sleep only to prepare me for another day of treatment at the hands of the followers of Sister Kenny.

Elizabeth Kenny had arrived in the United States from Australia in 1940. (She was not a nun; "sister" was the common courtesy title for nurses in Australia.) Her idea was simple and humane: Polio patients should not be kept immobile; their pain should be assuaged by moist heat, their muscles stretched out, and they should move. She was greeted with scorn or indifference by most of the American medical profession—so much so that she had decided to return to Australia, where she had established a clinic in 1933, when, at the last minute, some physicians at the Mayo Clinic in Minnesota let her give a demonstration of her technique to their staff. The staff was impressed and so they referred her to a polio hospital in Minneapolis, where she practiced for years afterward. Sister Kenny died just the year before I had polio, but by then her technique was in almost universal use, and she was thought of as a saint—even though her own therapeutic manner often lacked finesse.

Once our fevers subsided, most of us who had had polio were left with a body so rigid that to have someone lift our heel a quarter inch off the bed would produce excruciating pain. Thus the stretching part of the regimen was not begun until the hot packs had eased our stiffness somewhat. But even then, the stiffness was far from gone. One boy in Minneapolis who had the good fortune to be treated by Sister Kenny personally said that when he first met her, she came into the room—he guessed she was about six feet one, two hundred pounds or more—looked him in the eye, and said: "I'm here to try to help you. But, before I can help you, I've got to hurt you." Sister Kenny then reached over and lifted his left leg up off the bed. "I was damned if I was going to let anybody know how badly it hurt," he said later. "I wasn't going to yell, but the next thing I knew, I was crying from the pain." Sister Kenny noticed he was crying, so she put his left leg down and reached over and lifted his right leg and hurt him some more. "We won't do anything with your arms right now," Sister Kenny said; "I'll come back later this afternoon."

To another boy she treated, she said, "Pain is just a signal from your body that something is wrong. Once you recognize what is happening, you don't need to feel the pain anymore."

In Nebraska, a polio survivor named Robert Hall watched one of Sister Kenny's disciples stretch out the hamstrings of a fellow polio patient called Putzie by taking hold of Putzie's foot and just pushing down on it as hard as he could. "I could see beads of perspiration spring up on Putzie's forehead as he turned his head in pain. His deep draw for breath produced a faint whistle in his throat as the air rushed in. Then he screamed. I wonder how far the hair stood up on the back of my neck." The therapist didn't stop until he had the foot stretched straight out, maybe tearing some tissues. It took ten seconds. "Putzie was sobbing and gasping for breath. His whole body was heaving." So then the therapist let go of that foot and picked up the other one. "Putzie screamed again even louder this time. He was sobbing. He was just a heap in his chair . . . [and] I felt sick to my stomach."

My dear Mrs. Jones, who first came to my hospital room after I had done my two weeks with hot wet blankets, to begin stretching out my muscles, was far, far gentler—spreading out the pain in smaller increments over some weeks. She began every session with a massage, so that the stretching came gradually out of the massage, and, after the muscles had been stretched, they were soothed again afterward with another massage. She started just with my hands and feet, massaging and manipulating them a little bit, and she took some days before she had worked her way around to lifting my arms and legs an inch or two up off the bed. She worked gently, diligently, patiently to repair my body as much as she could and to dissolve my sense of hopelessness.

After this modest work of massage and stretching in my own room, which brought me to the point that it was not painful for me simply to be picked up and moved, I was deemed ready for the next stage of the therapy. Lifted out of bed onto a hospital cart, I was rolled through the corridor and into the elevator, down to the hospital basement, and into the physical therapy department, the domain of Mrs. Jones, who, with the help of a couple of strong male assistants, put me on a cloth stretcher, which was lowered by winch into a whirlpool bath the size and shape of an angel in the snow. There they turned on the warm water so that it churned over my body, whipping my loincloth into a frenzy, and, to my flustered embarrassment, bringing me to an orgasm within minutes.

Of course, I began to long for these sessions in the whirlpool bath. I told Mrs. Jones, every time I could work it naturally into the conversation, how much good I thought the whirlpool baths did me. And she ordered them for me way past the number of weeks usually allotted to this form of therapy. I was a model patient.

Others, who recovered in other hospitals, have told me that they were put into boiling hot tubs, left alone in vast, empty rooms, with cockroaches dropping from the ceiling into the water. This was not my experience. Buoyed by the water, I began gradually to be able to move my arms out from my sides, to bend my elbow and touch my face with my hand, to turn my head from side to side, to bring my hands together, to feel my stomach, my sides, my ribs, the unfamiliar terrain of my new body. My legs floated on their own in the water, swept wherever the currents would take them, but over the weeks, my left arm returned entirely to its former self, as strong as it had ever been. Even now, it's the only part of my body that feels as it did when I was fourteen.

Mrs. Jones was an old lady; well, maybe almost as old as I am now, at sixty. Small, with hardly any muscles of her own. Grandmotherly, I thought: gentle, partial to boys, very quiet and soothing, encouraging without buying any of the false optimism that was otherwise nearly universal. Whenever she said I was getting better, I believed her.

Big events, starting with the first and taking them in order: Becoming flexible enough to have my head propped up on pillows so that I could see around my whole room; this happened after a week of the hot-blanket treatment. Gradually being able to move the fingers of my right hand as well as those of my left, so that I saw there was life on both sides of my body; this happened in the last few days of the blankets. Then, being able to lift my left arm by myself off the surface of the bed, so that there was the prospect I might have something, at least one arm, to use to remake some sort of independent life; this after a week or ten days of Mrs. Jones's visits.

Then — a very big event, a moment of freedom — being able to turn over in bed by myself; this occurring after two weeks with Mrs. Jones, about a month after leaving the isolation ward. If you can turn over in bed, you are no longer entirely immobile.

And then things began to happen quickly: Sitting up in bed, supported by a half-dozen pillows to keep me from toppling over to the side, able to maintain a posture like that of a well person sitting in a chair or at a desk. Then, about six weeks after I had left the isolation ward, being able to sit up in a wheelchair and, gradually, finding I was able to move the wheels a little by myself, to go out into the corridor by myself, into the world. I was not bedridden. I could roll from room to room. In time, I could see, I would be able to get out onto sidewalks, into other buildings; be with people outside the hospital, have some kind of job, make some kind of life. A life in a wheelchair no longer seemed like a life of deprivation; from where I'd started it seemed a blessed liberation.

In the physical therapy department, lifting weights with my arms, building strength in my arms and shoulders so that, roughly two months after leaving the isolation ward, I was able to reach up and take hold of a metal bar fixed to the wall two feet above my head and pull myself up out of my wheelchair an inch or two, and then a dozen inches, and, finally, with Mrs. Jones and her strong aides there to catch me if I fell, with the aides holding my knees back for me so that they wouldn't buckle, I was able, swaying from side to side as I held on tightly to the metal bar, to pull myself up to something that looked almost vertical.

In Mrs. Jones's physical therapy department were a dozen pallets, where bodies could be laid out and worked over by a therapist, massaged, stretched, made to sit up, helped to do push-ups, rigged with weights and pulleys to do strength-building exercises. Long before the rest of the country spent its days in gyms and health clubs, I was there, developing a real hatred of exercise that has never left me.

This was in the days before guys went to exercise spas to hang out with sexy women in sleek workout clothes sipping bottled waters. In the therapy room at Sherman Hospital, there were no titanium weight machines painted jet black, no bright crimson stationary bicycles, no rock music, no articulated bodies glistening with oil, waiting around the health bar to see where idle conversation might lead. Our exercise stuff was made of black iron and stainless steel that looked like black iron and stainless steel—functional and bleak. We wore white cotton shirts and pants, all X-tra large, all too big: we did not look cool.

Electricity was still exciting to medical people back then, and so I was subjected to a little electrical stimulation, though nothing like the jolts of the olden days. I was told that the electrodes taped to my arms and legs and stomach would stimulate the nerves, reestablishing pathways that had blacked out, and/or that the electrical impulses would travel down a leg and make a toe move so that the doctors could at least see which pathways were still alive and thus maybe prove to be productive areas for muscle-building exercises.

So the electrodes were placed, I felt little mini-jolts of juice, the electrodes were taken up and placed again, taken up and placed again. This went on for several days, until I guess all my pathways had been stimulated. There was not much in the way of visible response to all this, so one day the doctors — feeling some embarrassment, I suppose — simply stopped showing up. I sensed the hopelessness well up again within me, and Mrs. Jones, perceptive as always, said casually that all that electricity business was quackery; that she and I would get my muscles back in shape with massage and exercise; and she set to work again patiently kneading my muscles.

I did table work every day, stretching, raising my arms and legs off the table with Mrs. Jones's help, getting gradually stronger until she would raise a leg and then let go as I tried to slow its descent back to the table. Many days passed like this, many with very little sense of progress. While I was lying on my back I worked out using small hand weights to exercise my forearms and biceps and, eventually, my shoulders. It was not possible to bring back to life any of the nerves that the virus had killed, and so the muscles that had once been activated by those nerves remained atrophied and useless. But not all the nerves were dead; some still sent messages out to muscles, and those muscles could be brought back and made to compensate, gradually, more or less, for the ones that were gone.

After the table work, I would be sat up in a chair in front of a set of horizontal bars attached to a wall, with my knees pressed against the lower bars to keep them from buckling, and I would pull myself up out of the chair to a standing position — assisted in this, as always, by Mrs. Jones and her strong aides who were there to catch me. Over and over again. I got better and better at this. Three months out of the isolation ward: My arms and shoulders were bulking up, ready to take over where they could for the muscles of the legs that would not come back. Not all the muscles of my arms came back to full strength. I learned different ways of raising an arm: turning my elbow in toward my rib cage, so that the muscles of my inner arm took over part of the work of the vanished muscle in my right shoulder, pulling my shoulder forward to call muscles into play from a different angle.

And I learned different ways of placing my weight on my feet when I stood, so that my posture, from shoulder down to heel, made a thousand tiny corrections for balance, and, with my knees locked in place against the horizontal bars, I could almost stand.

eight

At the far end of the workout room a space was left where a woman in an iron lung could be rolled in for a little therapy. I don't know who this woman was, and I never saw anything done to her.

This woman's fate was the fate of one in ten of those who were crippled by the polio virus: the disease struck the muscles of their diaphragm so that they couldn't breathe under their own power. Once the initial onslaught of polio stabilized, some people found they still had sufficient strength so that gradually, over a period of weeks or months, they could emerge from the iron lung—at first for a few hours at a time, then for longer periods, then forever. To help them in the transition, some of these people would be placed on a rocking bed, which slowly rocked like a teeter-totter: first the feet went up and the head went down, then the feet went down and the head went up, and in this way, the guts sloshed back and forth against the lungs and pushed air in and out to help them breathe.

Some of these people recovered sufficiently that they were able to leave both iron lung and rocking bed permanently behind. But some few never emerged from the iron lung, whether they lived for another few months or another forty years—

and this woman in the therapy department in Elgin was one of those few. Her fate was the grimmest of any of the polio patients' in the hospital. When she was rolled in to the therapy department, all activity stopped. There was silence. All of us had to think for a moment: That could have been my fate.

If you were in an iron lung and you wanted help, you couldn't reach for a bell, and chances were your voice wasn't loud enough for anyone to hear. So the woman in the iron lung developed a technique of making clicking sounds with her mouth, the sort of *tch-tch* you use to urge a horse along. The sharp clicking would cut through the wheezing sighs of the iron lung itself and carry through a ward or down a hall. I knew the woman in the lung was still alive if occasionally I heard her click. Or gulp. Sometimes, she would be taken out of the iron lung to see if she could make the escape to a rocking bed. And while she was out of the lung, she would also practice her frog breathing—swallowing air to force it down into her lungs, gulping it down, to try to learn to breathe in this way—until she started to fall behind and turn blue, and then she would be put back in the lung. I got to the point that I felt reassured when I came into the physical therapy room and heard either clicking or gulping.

The only time I saw the woman in the iron lung move was when she squirmed and squirmed for half an hour. All the muscles she had left were her neck muscles, and she managed to work her head and neck up further and further out of the iron lung until she got one of her shoulders partway out of the neck hole—which was when Mrs. Jones's assistants spotted her and stuffed her back in. Mrs. Jones went over to talk to her quietly for a while, gently, putting her hand in through one of the portholes on the side of the tank to stroke the woman's motionless arm. I never saw the woman try to escape again. Or maybe she was trying to commit suicide. After a couple of months, she died.

I had often seen visitors gather around the iron lung and talk to one another as though no one else were present. They would talk about her, and they would talk about others:

"Well, it looks as though he'll be able to get around pretty well on crutches; he's lucky not to end up in a wheelchair."

Or "Well, he's one of the lucky ones—at least he can get around in a wheelchair, you know; he's not in an iron lung."

Or "Well, probably she won't stay in that iron lung forever, and she's lucky to be alive."

Or "Well, it's lucky in a way—at least she didn't live on and have to spend the rest of her life in an iron lung."

This was my brief, but definitive, course in the absurdity of comparing my own life, and my own circumstances, to those of anyone else. We all have the experience of life in common, but the lives we all have are incomparable.

For sure, as President Kennedy liked to say, life is not fair. But it's even worse than that.

For those of us who had polio, it seemed inconceivable that such a life-transforming event could be random. If that were true, then no one is safe. Surely, some thought, *something* could have been done to prevent it; those who caught it must have been inattentive, or must have done something wrong, or—even more speculatively—perhaps they were being punished for having done something else wrong. That our lives could be so fragile, so subject to pure unreasoning luck, that our lives could be so far out of our control, that we could be so defenseless—this is unacceptable. Any cause is better than no cause at all. If there is no rational cause for what befalls us, if luck can begin and change and end our lives, then nothing lies beneath our feet but an abyss of complete meaninglessness: no pattern, no design, no logic, no coherence, nothing to count on, nothing to understand and master, no program to get with, no hope to shape our destinies. If this is true, then we are all absolutely vulnerable—and to accept that is horrifying. And yet this is exactly what I've come to believe is true.

The lives of others at the time I got polio:

At the age of six Edmund Sass was given injections of curare—the stuff South American jungle hunters dipped the tips of their arrows in to paralyze the animals they shot. Years later, Sass asked a doctor why anyone would have injected him with curare. The doctor smiled and said, "Well, it gave them something to do."

A nine-year-old girl named Marilynne Rogers, who got polio several years before I did, was given hot wax treatments. Children were covered with hot wax—presumably in a variation of the Sister Kenny method—and, to be sure, they screamed when the wax was removed and took all their body hair with it.

David Kangas, who got polio in 1952 at the age of fifteen and was still in the hospital doing physical therapy in the summer of '53, declined an invitation to go with a group of his companions when they managed to extricate themselves from the hospital to visit a faith healer who had come to town. "I remember them coming back from the healing tent and telling us what happened. They said that the preacher had put his hands on them and told them to rise and walk. But, of course, they couldn't. They were still in their wheelchairs when they got back."

But the medical profession is no more ready to give up on

patients than faith healers are. It may even be that the urge to do *something,* the refusal to acknowledge that there is nothing to be done, is a universal human instinct. It used to be said of Anthony Eden, who became prime minister of Great Britain for two years in 1955, that he could never resist the impulse to *do* something, even when doing nothing was clearly the better choice.

Around the same time I was in the hospital, Gail Bias, who got polio at the age two, had her first reconstructive surgery at age six, not knowing what it was for—something having to do with her feet. At the age of ten, she had her second surgery: her Achilles tendon was transplanted from the back of her heel to the top of her foot, to give her some lift for her toes when she walked. For her third surgery, "all the bones," she said, in her left foot were broken so that her foot would be "normal." Her fourth surgery came two weeks later, on her right leg: a "bone block," to keep that leg from growing more quickly than her polio-impaired left leg.

Kay Brutger had polio at the age of nine months. She had her first surgery for a drop foot when she was six years old. A plate was put in her right leg, an ivory screw in her right knee, and a cord was run down to her right foot to pull the toe up. After she recovered from the surgery, she still had a drop foot. She had her second surgery when she was eleven. Her right leg was not growing as quickly as her left leg, so they put staples in her left knee to slow the growth of her left leg. They also attempted to reposition her inward-turning left foot. After that surgery, she had a "trick" knee, and so, when she was seventeen, she was taken back into surgery to repair the knee. Eight screws and two plates were put in her knee and thigh. When she came out of the body cast six months later, she found her left foot had been set at the wrong angle so that she now had trouble walking both because of her drop foot and because of her inward turning left foot.

Bill Van Cleve, when he was able to get out of bed, where he'd been for about a year after contracting polio at age ten, found that his toes pointed outward, but the orthopedic surgeons at his hospital said, "Gee, we can fix this up. With a slice in the inner side of the arch we can remove a little bit of the tendon there, and that will cause the arch to curve up again." So the surgeons performed the procedure, but the surgery did not go quite as planned, and some complications ensued so that one leg grew to be a couple of inches shorter than the other one.

Pat Zahler, who had surgery at age six to fuse a bone in the left ankle, to "freeze" the ankle and prevent the characteristic polio drop foot, found that her left leg grew more slowly than her right leg, so she was taken back in for a second surgery, and her right knee was stapled to stunt the growth of her right leg, a procedure that was partially successful.

Sharon Kimball, who got polio at summer camp in 1953, when whe was nine, was taken in to surgery to cut loose a piece of the tensor fascia lata from the upper thigh, split it into two parts, bring one part up and tie it to a rib, and take the other part across her abdomen and tie it to her opposite hip arch. The idea was that this would stabilize her torso, to compensate for her weakened stomach muscles, so that she could lift her legs more easily to walk. Although the wounds healed, she said, the surgery wasn't especially successful, "unless you always intend to inhale. When you breathe in, the rib cage pulls back. But you also have to exhale." So, eventually, her surgeon suggested she wear a girdle.

For a curvature of her spine, Sharon was put into a body cast for a couple of months. This was done by suspending her from her head, to stretch out her spine, then putting on the plaster cast from her chin to below her hips. In order to eat, she had to stretch her chin up over the cast, which, her doctors explained, would stretch out her spine every time she ate.

After a few months, she was taken out of the cast for surgery, which involved chipping out little bits of pelvic bone and jamming them in between her vertebrae. One surgical procedure fused her lower spine; a second fused her upper spine.

Unfortunately, several months after surgery, her body cast cracked; the doctor suggested Sharon's mother patch it as best she could, and so her spinal fusion did not heal properly. She was taken in for surgery again, and spent the next five months in a cast in a hospital bed. When she was discharged from the hospital, having been in bed for a year, of course she couldn't walk at all, though, in time, she taught herself to walk at home, pushing a chair around the kitchen.

Barb Johnson, who had polio at the age of three, had her first surgery at age five—for what, she doesn't know, although she has scars along the sides of her feet. She had her second surgery at age ten, to have pins inserted in her left knee to slow the growth of that leg. For her third surgery, she had a "V-fistula," to increase the rate of growth in her right leg. This was done by taking a vein and attaching it to an artery to enhance the blood flow in that leg. A couple of years later, she had surgery to undo the V-fistula, because it was judged to be putting an undue strain on her heart. When she woke up from the anesthetic after one of these surgeries—she doesn't remember which one—she does remember that the first thing she said was, "I'm not crying, Mom!"

When she was fifteen, some surgery was done on the bones of her right foot, and something was done with the tendons of that foot to try to give some lift to her toes. When the toe surgery failed, she returned to the hospital to have a bone chip taken from her shin, to be fused into her toe to keep it straight. Now, "even though the surgeries were successful," she says, she walks with a slight limp, has different-size feet—she wears a size 6 shoe on one foot and a size 4½ on the other—and different-length legs, and she tends to stub the fused toe quite a lot. "I think I got through high school pretty well," she says. "I didn't date, and I didn't go to school dances . . . but otherwise, I did pretty much everything everyone else did."

I think about these stories, and I thank God my parents didn't let one surgeon after another try his luck on me.

nine

And yet, as frightening as idle surgeons were, they were nothing compared to the occupational therapists. One day, I was wheeled out onto a sunporch, a place painted bright yellow, with flowered curtains: the occupational therapy room. Here I saw a half-dozen or so figures heaped into their wheelchairs—children who had had polio, and older folks who had had strokes—learning to perform tasks that would help them to lead independent lives: weaving baskets, punching holes in leather belts, making a macramé key chain. I don't think I ever saw anything more alarming.

Some people worked laboriously in clay, to strengthen their hands even as they practiced a useful craft. One elderly man was writing something, his arm suspended in a sling from a metal contraption attached to his wheelchair: in the hour I spent on the sunporch, he would finish almost half a page. I saw a middle-aged woman praised with extravagant enthusiasm by a therapist after she had managed to eat a bowl of Jell-O all by herself. I saw a man who was probably in his fifties, trying to learn to tie his shoe.

So what lay in store for me now? Would I seek employment as a maker of key chains? I struggled not to scorn the artisans of macramé and ashtrays and beaded purses—pathetic old wrecks of men and women whose strokes had left them paralyzed and drooling. I lectured myself not to look down on the abilities of others, just as I would not wish others to look down on my abilities; to recognize that we all bring the gifts we can to the world and need to respect one another's gifts. But even so, as I looked around the sunporch, the sheer terror of coming so close to having such limited abilities for the rest of my life triggered some deep inner voice to yell at me to run, just as it yells at others to run from me, just as I see, these days, little children back away from me when I come near. Grown-ups have learned to repress this response, but children are honestly frightened of what they might catch from me, just as I was frightened at what I might catch from these ruined people in the occupational therapy room.

Just a year before, on entering high school, and like all incoming freshmen, I was given a test by the school's guidance counselor, to see where my talents and tastes might lie. The Kuder Vocational Preference Test was not an aptitude test, but rather an "attitude" test, one that was extremely popular in the fifties, when it was presumed that what mattered most in predicting how you would do in the world was what kind of guy you were, who you got along with, what was congenial to you, whether you were the sort of person who preferred, say, staying home alone reading books or going out with friends to a movie on Saturday night. (These tests were not hard to pass, but I remember that if you got a score of less than 37 or more than 44, there would be some reason "for doubting the value of your answers." My score was 42.)

I ranked fairly low in my interests in the outdoors and in mechanical things, moderately high in computational and scientific matters, fairly high in the arts of persuasiveness (this interest, I was told, would be common to actors, politicians, radio announcers, ministers, and salesmen). I ranked fairly high in my interest in artistic things, extremely high in musical interests. From this, the Kuder people and my guidance counselor suggested that I should be a dentist, a pharmacist, or a radio sound engineer—all fine professions although, it seemed to me, a little remote from music. I thought the Kuder people were just sort of funny and harebrained, but I thought the occupational therapists on the sunporch were trying to put a boot on my chest and suffocate me.

They encouraged me to come back every day; they thought, I suppose, that, if it came to that, macramé might be a useful skill for me. The nurses who cared for me in the children's ward also encouraged me to go to occupational therapy each day—and took my resistance to joining in with the happy group as evidence that I was not recovering emotionally; they took it as a refusal to get better, or as a form of depression. It didn't occur to them that I could only consider recovering into a life different from the one the therapists offered me. Ever since that time—or maybe even before that time—I haven't been good at joining, especially if the group to be joined seems to me a little too cheerful.

What would it mean anymore, by the way, to recover? That I would recover my former self, with all the possibilities that were open to me when I took the Kuder Vocational Preference Test?

One boy's father kept a faithful record of his son's experience of polio. This passage from it sounds like an absolute distillation of the way we spoke in the fifties:

"Charlie," [the therapist] said, "you want to be completely well again, don't you?"

"Yes, ma'am, I sure do. I want to go to summer camp next year."

"All right, then. Whatever I tell you to do, you must do. And work, work all the time. Can I count on you to cooperate with me?"

"Gosh," he spilled out. "I'll do anything."

Americans have always been can-do people. Having just emerged from World War II, we were maybe more can-do than ever.

One mother was doing all she knew how to encourage her son to put his will into recovering. There was a fellow in Virginia, she told her son, who was told he would never walk again, but he worked hard and learned to walk with "just a little bit of a limp." That fellow, the boy's mother said, "just made up his mind he was going to do it himself."

Another mother, whose son recovered almost entirely, explained it this way: "It was his own wanting to and fighting against it that did it. He'd just talk about when he came home he was going to ride his bike, and, by gosh, he did."

In her biography of her friend Bea Wright, who had had polio, Eleanor Chappel wrote that Wright "was no sanctimonious weakling resolving to silently bear her burden, but a woman who refused to accept what had happened as a locked door." Bea Wright knew that there was a "right way" to deal with polio, and that was to fight. Polio was "the most tangible enemy she had faced yet, and she intended to give it 'no quarter.' "

The moral of these stories was clear to us at the time: The way to win was to fight; the fight was up to us; and it was a test of character. The penalty for failure was to be a helpless invalid for life. On the other hand, success would be greeted not simply as a good thing, but as a wonderful and deeply sat-isfying thing. The improvement that young polio patients showed, as Fred Davis wrote in his book *Passage Through Crisis,* was "a miniature reenactment of the classic American success story," and stories like these added "to our culture's ample storehouse of myths, tales, and 'known instances' of man's tri-umphing over seemingly impossible circumstances to prove that it is he and he alone who fashions his fate."

The good thing about identifying with the hokey, swag-gering, easy loping John Wayne World War II ethos that per-meated the country in the fifties was that most of us who had polio didn't feel like victims. We felt like survivors, even heroes. A young fellow named Arnold Beisser who had been a naval reserve doctor and a tennis player when he got polio in 1950—and was left a quadriplegic in a motorized wheelchair who needed mechanical assistance with his breathing—de-cided to think of his disability as a "competitive sport," and charted his recovery day by day as though it were a training program.

The ethos of the time affected the caretakers as well as their patients—which I think explains a good deal of the happily doled out, gratuitous toughness on the part of a lot of the doc-tors and nurses. I remember one time, after I was beginning to get flexible enough to bend my neck and have a pillow under my head, that I was troubled by the softness of my new pil-low. I still hadn't the strength to turn my head against the feather pillow and asked the nurse if there might be a harder pillow I could have. When the doctor made his rounds that day, the nurse told him I'd asked for a harder pillow, and he said, "Fine, sure. Get him a brick." And gave me a quick, fellow-Marine smile before he sauntered out the door.

Girls were treated no less gruffly than boys. An eleven-year-old girl who got polio a few years before I did was sent to the D. T. Watson Home for Crippled Children in Pittsburgh, where "a nurse came in and gave me a plate with spaghetti on it, and I was totally paralyzed . . . She said, 'We're not going to coddle you here. You'll have to eat your dinner.' And I couldn't reach it. . . . I'll always remember that. And then she came in and took it away."

And girls as well as boys learned to be tough themselves. A seven-year-old named Dorothy Pallas said she never complained of the painful stretching routines she was put through for "fear of being called a quitter and a coward, the one who couldn't take it."

But the deepest influence of all was probably not the postwar culture. It was, rather, as Kathryn Black has written, "the need to believe that human will can overcome *anything*." To believe that things can't just happen to you and be irrevocable.

Daniel J. Wilson, an associate professor of history at Muhlenberg College in Pennsylvania, did an analysis in 1994 of the autobiographies of people who had had polio. He read fifty stories. Almost all of them, he said, are "accounts of triumph over adversity," triumphs of "will power and hard work."

This basic narrative of triumph came with a required character description, too, what the physician and ethicist Howard Brody has called the "good handicapped person," a person who makes every possible effort to regain an independent, self-supporting life for himself, who, against great odds, works at a job we find surprising a handicapped person is able to perform, makes a successful career, never mentions his disability, never betrays any suggestion of self-pity, and never displays an attitude that suggests passive acceptance of or resignation about his handicap. On the contrary, his life is dedicated to a positive, energetic struggle that seeks out every opportunity for normality. The editor of a publication of the Association for the Aid of Crippled Children added to this prescription the rubric that there was a special taboo against bitterness which required the handicapped person to "express his pain, his desires, his hope, and his anguish only in the most superficial manner; if he expresses his bitterness deeply or with any sense of personal tragedy, he risks alienating the nonhandicapped."

Every boy and girl at Sherman Hospital knew this was what was expected, this was the story and the character that needed to be enacted. These were not lessons that had to be learned over a long life; they were so deeply, pervasively embedded in the culture that they were instantly available to any kid in a hospital bed.

Now of course, these writers knew, as I did, people who died. A couple of days before Robert Hall was discharged from the hospital, he noticed that a fourteen-year-old boy had been brought in with bulbar polio. "It looked bad right from the start. He was in the iron lung room for special treatment," Hall wrote. Hall returned to the hospital every afternoon for his own physical therapy and kept track of the boy. One day he was told the boy had had to have a tracheotomy, that he had almost died the night before, and his parents and a priest had been there most of the night. Bulbar usually killed quickly, but this boy seemed to be rallying. The common wisdom was that the longer you stayed alive, the better your chances for making it. On his way out of the hospital that afternoon, Hall looked in on the boy, who was having a hard time breathing. "He hadn't learned to relax yet with the bubbles going down the red tube bringing life to him. I wondered if he [knew] what it was all about. From the set expression on his face and the look in his eyes—and I could see mile after mile into those eyes—I could tell he was a fighter. . . . I wanted to tell him I was pulling for him."

Over the next couple of days, the boy lost ground and rallied, lost ground and rallied. And then, one day when Hall got off the hospital elevator for his therapy, "I was stopped cold by the sickening odor of the disinfectant. For a moment, I was stunned cold." He hoped his instincts were wrong, but then he saw: "the iron lung was out in the hall again." The boy was dead. Fighting hadn't mattered.

And there were people who, at least at first, couldn't, or wouldn't fight. Leonard Kriegel hated the idea of having to walk with braces and crutches, which was, for him, the very image of being a cripple. "At first, the war was between Mr. Thompson and me. Mr. Thompson was the therapist in charge of rehabilitation, and he coddled me with the textbooks that told him to ascribe to fear my refusal to cooperate with his desires for me. But it wasn't fear. It was hatred, hatred of what they were trying to make of me, and I knew it. . . . I refused to think of walking. I thought of it as necessity, as doing what they wanted me to do. I was meeting them halfway, but at the same time I was matching my will against theirs, my knuckle-down boyhood shrewdness against their closed-fist adult power. I never took more than five or six steps."

"I wondered," wrote Edward Le Comte, "whether I had the right character to be 'rehabilitated'—a term normally applied to social deviants. I disliked intensely the moralizings that were flung at us. 'Mary did it—you can do it.' Didn't it depend on how much of either of us the virus had eaten? But, as is likely to happen with incessant propaganda, some of it stuck. Maybe there were indeed borderline cases where, 'whether you ever walk again is *up to you!*'" And then, when he had recovered some of his abilities, Le Comte wrote, "I should have been exhilarated . . . [but] I was only depressed. The road ahead was longer and rougher than my worst imaginings, the mirror at the end of the parallel bars [where he held himself steady on his feet to learn to walk again] hopelessly distant; and reaching that—sometime in the fifth month—would only be the beginning of the beginning."

Joan Hardee came out of an iron lung at last, able to breathe on her own, and then—having taken this immense step toward recovery—saw how far she was in fact from normal life, and despaired. "I knew that I would not die, and could not, even though I wished it. I slumped into a great depression with no positive wish or will about anything."

At some point Larry Alexander realized that, in fact, he would never walk again, no matter how hard he fought, that nothing could be done for his "helpless flesh and bone," but that, even so, it had to be "kept alive, nursed and cared for the way a baby is cared for." He slipped into a deep depression; he lost all interest in reading, talking, therapy. "I had no grip on life, no logical reason to go on living. You'd be better off dead."

And there are other stories of those who were left bedridden for life, who didn't make it, who couldn't overcome their disabilities no matter how hard they tried, who lived on in iron lungs and never came to feel courageous and accepting about it. But their stories aren't available to us—because they didn't know how to tell them in a way that could fit the way the culture said the stories should be told, or because no one wanted to hear them, no one wanted to publish them or put them on television. In 1961, a survey was done of 806 people with long-term disabilities from polio: 29 percent of them could not feed themselves; 31 percent could feed themselves only with assistive devices; 83 percent could not get dressed by themselves; 32 percent could not write; 40 percent could not get from bed to wheelchair without help; nearly 50 percent could not propel a wheelchair by themselves. For many people, as Paul Bates has written, "Having polio is to be forced to do nothing, for there seems to be nothing you can do; to have polio is to stare at the ceiling; to have polio is to do nothing for yourself; to have polio is to fight with a disease which would, if it could, rob you of the ability to do anything, presenting you with each twenty-four hours as a barren waste with no choice but to endure them."

If a girl spends her life in an iron lung, we want to hear how she triumphed over it, how she became a deeper, better, wiser, more profoundly philosophical and transcendent person for it; how, in fact, it was almost a wonderful advantage to spend a life in an iron lung, because of the insight it yielded. We like success. We can't bear failure. We don't want to hear about it. I don't. I can't bear a story of failure—unless it ends tragically: a person dies; it is immensely sad; we mourn, we recognize our mortality; we grieve for human destiny; we feel pity and terror; we are purged; and then we forget the person, and we get on with our lives. But for a person to linger forever, as so many do, never recovering, never coming to terms with his fate, to fail, to become a lifelong invalid, unable to care for himself, incapable of rising to the daily challenge of futile effort, overcome by bitterness or despair, needy of public assistance, homeless, good for nothing but to provide a living specimen for young interns being trained in the emergency rooms of inner-city hospitals to practice on—this is unbearable; depressing; a daily reminder of just how vulnerable we all are. We don't need it. We don't want it. We hope we will never find a use for these stories.

There is something to be said for this willful ignorance: We don't need to learn how to fail in our lives; we need to learn how to succeed. We don't want to identify with failure, to rehearse failure, to feel comfortable with it, to get good at it. We want to rehearse success; we want to know what qualities of character are needed for triumph.

The notion that any problem can be solved with will, determination, and ingenuity certainly helped build the strong, powerful nation America had become by the time I got polio. It continues to inspire successful, expansive business enterprises and individual lives. It helps people get through the day. It sent my father out to work every morning with the feeling that his efforts were going to be rewarded. It gave a lift to his spirits, an energy to his life, a faith in the future, and he worked hard and happily in the sustenance of that belief.

And yet the refusal to recognize the possibility of failure, the refusal to accept the tragic nature of life and the knowledge that all problems do not have solutions, all this came to constitute more than a mere metaphysical error in America. It produced an entire subculture of denial and shame, where failure cannot be admitted, where those who cannot succeed must apologize and take the blame, where a vast network of institutions has been built to hide the millions who cannot pull themselves up by their own bootstraps, a culture in which failure is swept under the rug, where death is denied, where we undertake extravagant attempts to fix the unfixable in hospital operating rooms and in sovereign countries such as Vietnam, and where those who object to this must feel themselves judged to be wanting, to be neurotic, losers, not quite good Americans, not quite psychologically robust, needing a change in their diet, their vitamins, their aerobic conditioning, their meditation techniques, their outlook on life, where we know to say of someone who doesn't go along with the program: Well, of course, you know, he's been psychologically damaged.

This culture made me feel, as a boy, that I needed to keep my chin up, reassure my parents about how well I was doing, never be sad, look to the future, be optimistic, perform a can-do persona even if I felt no connection to it. It made me live a lie, confuse myself about who I was and what I felt and how life was for me. I was disoriented, with no guideposts that seemed reliable or even sane; I had to adjust to a world I thought was crazy. I learned to lie to my parish priest and my football coach and my parents, who didn't seem to know, or couldn't bring themselves to admit, the truth they saw before their very eyes.

As a country, America was forced in the 1960s to ac-knowledge, in part, the limitations of its wonderful, robust mythology—to take more the tragic view of life that many other, older nations have come to live with, to recognize that some things cannot be done, some things cannot be fixed; that at some moment, even if it is only in the final moment, every-one is crushed by life; that in the end, we don't come through life as we hope to, richer and stronger and smarter; in the end, no matter who we are, we are all completely shattered and consumed by life.

And yet, meanwhile, in truth, we all still need a little de-nial to get through our days.

One little boy, seven years old, with both legs in heavy steel braces, asked his Little League coach if he could play that year. The coach, thrown off guard, said all the positions were filled that season but he should think about playing the following year. The boy told his mother: "I'll be playing with the Little Leaguers next year."

H. C. A. Lassen, the chief of the department of communicable diseases at Blegdam Hospital in Copenhagen in the early 1950s, believed that patients who were being successful at denying the gravity of their condition should not have their hopes shattered by telling them too much about their odds for full recovery: It is, he said, "practically never too late for the patient to realize he is a respirator patient for life."

Really, even the story of Franklin Roosevelt was not one of *physical* triumph. As Kathryn Black has pointed out, Roosevelt tried "massage, saltwater baths, ultraviolet light, electric currents, parallel bars as supports [for walking], horseback riding, an electric tricycle, exercises in warm water and cold water, osteopathy, and every manner of muscle training. He exercised in the morning and practiced walking in the afternoon [for seven years]. Despite all that effort, time, and expense, he never managed more than a few tortured steps supported by braces, a cane, and the strong arm of someone else. In fact, he never even stood up, except for speeches, receptions, and military reviews."

President Roosevelt, many years after he had had polio, still told his family and friends that he was expecting to recover completely in another couple of years.

ten

The goal was to be a real person who could walk. Walking was the whole deal.

"He'll never walk again" was the ultimate killer Hollywood movie line.

And whenever you did see someone begin to walk again—so awkward, fragile, and dangerous an enterprise—it seemed a miracle.

The common dream—and it was my dream, too—was that one day we would just get up and walk again, like a real miracle, like making a pilgrimage to Lourdes and being cured by the holy waters there. And sometimes something like that did happen. Something close to a miracle happened for eighteen-year-old Robert Gurney, who had been in the hospital about eleven months when one day his physical therapist said to him, "When we're done with your exercises today, you're going to walk around this table."

Robert was incredulous; he said he couldn't do it.

"Don't think about it," his therapist said; "just do it."

So Robert did.

His therapist said, "See, you can do it."

But Robert said, "Yeah, but I was holding on to the table."

The therapist said, "I don't care whether you were holding

on or not. . . . You're not going back to your room in a wheel-chair, you're going to walk back. I'm going to help you, but you're going to walk back."

So they walked, with the therapist's arm around Robert's shoulder. And as he went down the hall, his friend Henry called out from a room, "Hey, Bobby, you're walking."

"Yeah," Robert said. "Bill's helping me."

"Bill who?"

"You know, Bill, my therapist."

"Where is he?"

Robert looked around; he was by himself. Bill was halfway back the corridor talking to some nurses. Robert was walking by himself!

He took three more steps forward, and two steps back, and fell to the floor laughing. And then Henry was laughing so hard he was crying.

Or there was the way—not so much like a miracle—that it happened for sixteen-year-old Ray Gullickson, one of Sister Kenny's boys, who happened to roll quietly in his wheelchair into the room where the physicians kept their patients' files. Ray found his own file and read the doctor's opinion that he would not walk for a year, and when he did, he would always need a leg brace. He was shocked and determined to prove the doctor wrong. "Late that evening, after they had turned off most of the lights in the [ward], I grabbed the edge of my bed with my left hand and lowered myself onto the floor to see if I could stand up. I was very weak, and I wondered if this was such a good idea. Standing for the first time . . . gave me quite a sensation. . . . I broke out in a cold sweat, and I started to shake." He knew he was in danger of falling, so, after a little while, he climbed back into bed.

He repeated this routine every night for more than a week, standing a little longer each time. "Within 10 days or so, I was able to take a step. A few days after that, I was able to walk completely around the end of my bed." He kept practicing every night on his own.

And then one Sunday afternoon, sitting in his wheelchair, he saw his girlfriend Carol walking toward him. "I forgot I was in a wheelchair, stood up, and walked over to the sun porch to meet her. It was the first time anyone had seen me walk, and I'm not sure who was the most excited: Carol, Sister Kenny, or me! I made it as far as the doorway, but then I collapsed. . . .

"The doctor and the nurses seemed totally exasperated . . . they sure weren't very careful when they picked me up and dropped me into the wheelchair. . . .

". . . Sister Kenny didn't say anything. She just reached over and put her hand on my shoulder, and I could tell that she was delighted by what I had done."

The way it happened for me was that first, I practiced, by grabbing hold of the horizontal bars that were attached to the wall, pulling myself up out of my wheelchair to my feet and trying to stand there holding on, my midsection swaying from side to side, my knees giving out from time to time, as I learned to bring myself back to equilibrium with the muscles that were ordinarily used for this purpose and with whatever other muscles my body could imagine calling into play to compensate for those that were gone. This was the new equilibrium, a bizarre, jury-rigged system of muscular checks and balances that could not be taught. The body had to learn this on its own through days and days of trial and error.

And while the body tried to discover some new ways of

holding itself upright, the legs had to discover how to keep the knees from buckling. There were the usual thigh muscles to be strengthened, which keep the knees locked in place. But there were ways to shift one's weight, too, and to cheat by pulling back the buttocks to alter the angle at which the body's weight came down on the joint. And if none of these strategies were sufficient, then technology and brute force came into play in the form of braces.

I was able to hold my right knee in place when I stood on my right leg, but my left knee buckled no matter what I did. And so the bracemakers were called in to measure me, and they fashioned a device that had two thick strips of steel to go down along each side of my left leg. These steel strips were held together by several steel crossbars and by leather straps. Halfway down the leg, at the knee, a hinge allowed the brace to bend so that I could sit down. When I stood, I slid a little steel band down onto the hinge to lock it in place. My knee was held firm and unbending by a leather pad. And the low ends of the steel strips went down past my ankle and were anchored into a special shoe. In this way, my left knee could no longer bend when I stood.

As clumsy and brutal and heavy and medieval as the technology of this apparatus was, I thought it was clever—and it worked. Not long after I got this brace, once I'd practiced standing by holding on to the wall of horizontal bars, Mrs. Jones got me up for my first step. She and three of her strong-armed assistants sat me up on a cot and swung my steel-clad leg over the side. Like Frankenstein. Then the four of them, one holding me around the waist, one under each armpit, one in front waiting for me to fall, hoisted me to my feet and held me there. Like the Marx Brothers. Then they tilted me forward and lifted me up at the waist on my left side only so that that foot came off the floor, and my steel leg swung forward absurdly, and Mrs. Jones cried out: "There! You've taken your first step!"

This was three months and five days after Mrs. Fuller carried me into the isolation ward.

Not quite like Gurney or Gullickson, but I was on my way. From this first step, Mrs. Jones judged me ready for the parallel bars. And so, on the day appointed for me to try adding a second and a third step to my first, my wheelchair was pushed over to one end of the bars. These were standard-issue gym equipment, maybe ten or twelve feet long, an unimaginable distance from where I sat all the way down to the far end of the bars. I was pulled up out of the wheelchair and propped against the near end of the bars so that I could reach out and get a grip on them. My assignment then was to throw myself forward, holding on to the bars, and drag and fling and scuffle my feet forward a little at a time, and in this way lurch from one end to the other. This first time out, I knew I would not make it to the end. I was expected to be able to take a few "steps," and then the gaggle of Mrs. Jones's helpers would maneuver the wheelchair under the bars and come up behind me and lower my wobbling, exhausted, jellylike body back into the chair while they praised me and marveled at my success.

And just that previous winter, at the ice-skating rink, I'd had to fall down on purpose, to pretend I couldn't skate so perfectly, to show that I could make mistakes, too, so that the others would let me join their game of hockey.

We worked five days a week, Mrs. Jones and I: stretching, working with light free weights, pulling myself up to my feet on the horizontal bars attached to the wall, and then — the peak moment—pulling myself up between the parallel bars to walk, until I was able to make it to the end of the bars and back again.

And then, although I was still unsteady on my feet, and held on to those parallel bars with all my strength, Mrs. Jones decided it was time to break this dependence on the bars, to cut loose and work without a net: to walk with crutches.

Once again surrounded by my team of therapist friends, one in front, one in back, one on each side, I placed one crutch an inch or two forward and heaved and slid the opposite foot forward, getting it stuck a little sideways, needing my port-side crew member to straighten it out, and in this way, after two or three weeks, I was able to scuttle my way crablike on my own down the smooth, polished floors of the corridor outside the therapy room.

My first crutches were the familiar wooden ones. But I was told they would not do for the long term: the pressure of the wood against the nerves in my armpits would finally cause numbness in my hands. So I was given a pair of "Canadian" crutches: aluminum tubes fitted with a handle and with a cuff that went around the forearm to hold it steady. These were trickier to learn to use than the wooden ones but not as clumsy once I got the hang of them.

Of course, these Canadian crutches were unbelievably ugly. Indeed, hospital equipment in general is remarkably ugly, and for no reason I can think of other than that the sick ought to be punished. In the fifties, automobiles had fins, bright chrome, dazzling colors; men wore beautiful cravats from Jacques Fath, Hawaiian shirts, elegant double-breasted suits, wing-tip shoes; women wore ostrich feathers in their hats, gowns designed by Dior and Chanel. But wheelchairs and crutches were designed as though they were intended for prisoners in Siberia. They were functional and ugly and depressing. Certainly there were enough people on crutches at the time to provide a market for something cool. But designer crutches have only recently appeared; I snapped up one of the new designs just three years ago: sleek, lightweight, fire engine red.

One day Robert Hall's therapist told him he should walk to physical therapy the following morning and leave his wheelchair behind in his room. So Robert dutifully set out the next morning on foot. He managed to get out of his room well enough, by holding on to his bed and a chair and other pieces of furniture. But once he got into the corridor there was no longer anything to hold on to. After three steps, he fell down. As it happened, his therapist and a couple of others were on the sunporch and turned to look when he hit the floor. But none of them moved to help him. There was nothing in the corridor to grab to pull himself up, and he felt his anger rising against the three men watching him from the sunporch. He dragged himself to a wall and sat with his back to it, his legs stretched out in front of him. Putting his palms flat against the wall, he pushed his body up the wall inch by inch, his heels holding him uncertainly each stage of the way, slipping back to the floor again and again and, each time, starting over, becoming angrier and angrier. Finally, he got to his feet, leaning against the wall. He rested a moment and started off down the corridor again. After four steps, he fell once more, the men on the sunporch still watching him. Once more he slid himself over to the wall, and inched his way up, and started off walking—and fell. After a while, his therapist and the others left the sunporch and walked on ahead to the therapy room, not turning back to look at him as he inched his way up the wall again.

He fell thirty-six times getting to physical therapy that morning. By the time he arrived there, he said, he had learned how to fall properly, and how to use a wall to get back up. His therapist was busy when Robert got to the therapy room, but, a little later in the day, the therapist said to him, casually, "You made it."

Of all the lessons of polio, Robert Hall asked, what is the greatest? And answered, without hesitation: Patience. Patience beyond any normal patience. And then, more patience. And after that: real, deep patience. And then, from time to time, usually over the most trivial of things—a shoelace that will not tie easily, a shoe that will not slip smoothly onto the foot—flaring wild raging impatience.

And what is the most constant companion? Longing.

After just three weeks of practice, I was able, with my brace and my crutches, to walk the full length of the hospital corridor outside the physical therapy department—about fifty or sixty feet.

Mrs. Jones and her strong-armed boys, having taught me how to walk, coached me on how to fall, how to twist to the side as I was going down so that I could catch myself with the strength of an arm and roll with the fall. I remembered football practice, the afternoons we'd spent learning to roll. Falling, being knocked down, the coach had said, was an inevitable part of football; we had to learn to do it well so we wouldn't be injured. I've taken a lot of falls since then: There is the familiar toe catch—on a crack in the pavement, or an uneven doorjamb—that accounts for most of the falls I take now. And there is the occasional sudden break of a crutch's supportive forearm cuff that will send me abruptly sideways. That one is hard to defend against, and is the reason I don't walk close to the edge of a subway or train platform. The other fall that is hard to defend against is the one where someone innocently comes from behind and kicks the crutch out from under me. I go down fast on that one. The pocket grabber—in which my trouser pocket unaccountably takes hold of the handle of my crutch—will send me lurching sideways. It's not easy remembering all these little dangers and, at the same time, carrying on a conversation with a companion as you walk down a street. The worst threat may be, in the middle of a conversation, to step off a curb and put a crutch tip down into a sewer grating in the street; that mistake once tossed me like a judo throw, and that's a mistake you don't make twice. Large clothing—a raincoat, an overcoat, a bulky winter coat—will grab hold of a crutch and fling me to the ground, too.

I have an abiding fear of high places; any high place strikes me simply as a place from which to fall. Once, I visited a friend of Bets's who lived in Chicago in a new skyscraper designed by Mies van der Rohe. It was a beautiful building. When we got off the elevator and went into the apartment, I crumpled immediately to the floor, like an old soldier hearing an explosion and dropping instinctively onto his belly. Mies had designed these apartments so that each living room had a picture window running from floor to ceiling and wall to wall—with the glass set at an angle so that it was completely invisible, so that it looked as though there were no window or wall there, just a thousand-foot drop into Lake Michigan.

I feel fairly certain that I'm fated to die by falling onto a subway track—because of a crutch snapping, or someone inadvertently bumping me off balance—so I always take cabs, postponing the inevitable day I don't have cab fare and ride the subway just that one time.

I fear large crowds, of course, and always pick my way very slowly through a cocktail party, braced at all times against an inadvertent shove from any direction—trying, as I do this, to make the stately manner of my progress look intentional and dignified rather than defensive. When I move through a crowd of schoolchildren, I speak in a loud happy voice to all the kids, and make conversation with all of them so that they can see me coming and not plow me under with a sudden move.

The knowledge that comes from your own body is certain knowledge. To know things in your bones, in your muscles and sinews, is to know things beyond question. I know some things absolutely: I know there are definitive things in life, final things, things that do not change, things you cannot take back. Some things, once done, are done forever.

I know there are limits; I know false hopes are not to be nurtured.

At the same time, I know the immense possibilities of compensation; I know the necessity of flexibility, the need to look for unexpected combinations of things, the need to be slow to reach final conclusions; I know that even if the realities are fixed, the relationships among them, the ways of dealing with them, are completely open and unfixed.

You can get cocky in a hospital; sliding your feet along the polished floor, you can think you've become quite the accomplished pedestrian. I thought I had, and I wanted to go home. I thought I was more than ready.

Mrs. Jones disagreed—but very gently and tentatively, and only partially. She thought I might have forgotten how rough the sidewalk pavement was. She was worried that if I made too early an attempt on the outside world, I might fail and become demoralized. But finally, in early October, she thought it might be good for me to go home for a weekend visit.

My mother and father and Bets all came to drive me home. The car was brought to the emergency room door, and I was wheeled out to within ten feet of the car and hoisted to my feet.

Then, suddenly, I thought I'd never make it quite all the way: just outside the emergency room door was asphalt, whose rough surface, after the smooth corridors of the hospitals, was indeed a shock, and I wondered immediately if I could survive on the outside. But Mrs. Jones was with me—standing right next to me as we looked across this chasm of asphalt—and she said to me, quietly, "We can make it." And so we did, all the way to the car.

As I turned around next to the open car door, someone took my crutches as I handed them off without looking and, with three or four people helping and bracing me, I lowered myself backward onto the front seat, reached down to unlock my brace, swung my legs up and into the car; someone closed the door. Settled in the car, I found I was smiling.

The ride itself—back through the rolling hills and open fields of what had come to seem like early boyhood, places I thought I might never go again—was wonderful. But it had been so long since I had seen sky and trees and felt breeze coming in through a car window that I had to turn my head away from the others in case tears came to my eyes.

Once we pulled up and stopped in the driveway, I saw an obstacle I had never anticipated: about fifteen feet of well-trimmed grass, the shortcut between the car and the house. The grass seemed extraordinarily high to me, the ground fiendishly uneven with all its minuscule hillocks and valleys, all the little nuances that are ordinarily invisible to the casual lawn crosser.

It took me half an hour to get across the grass; once again I thought I'd have to give up and be picked up and carried. My father asked if I wanted him to carry me in. And that's when Bets stepped between me and my parents, not allowing their grief to disable me. She had seen a lot of World War II movies about returning war heroes who were tough, and who got on with their lives, who refused to sink under the weight of self-pity and the pity of others, people who defined themselves not by their weaknesses but by their strengths, guys who wore their battle scars with pride. Bets said: "Leave him alone. He can make it."

My father had built a pair of parallel bars onto the side porch so that I could lift myself up to the porch rather than have to go up the four front steps to the house. I was drenched in sweat by the time I got to the parallel bars, but I swung up on those with no trouble at all, and then made the few smooth feet across the porch to the threshold of the door into the living room. There I was defeated. The threshold was three-quarters of an inch high. I stopped and considered my options, running different possible solutions through my mind. Then I dropped the crutches and simply threw myself forward, catching myself with my hands as I fell — pretending, as everyone gasped and cried out, that this was the way I always went through a door — and dragged myself across the living room rug to hoist myself up onto the couch, home at last. For a weekend.

eleven

I luxuriated in my home that weekend. I sat on the leather couch and absorbed the familiar living room again with each one of my senses, drawing the room back into myself, all its scents and shapes, the dimensions of its walls, the flowered upholstery, the curve of the polished legs of the tall end table, the pale green table lamp at one end of the couch, the brass tray on the coffee table, icy cold to the touch even in Indian summer, the painting of two draft horses pulling a wooden plow, guided by a farmhand through a field — all these things returned me to my home, a center for my life, a place to be and to go out from, to know who I was, where I came from, to have some security in my past, some sense of going on, and to have all this texture of life that I didn't know I had been missing in the hospital, the stuff of life on earth.

And I sat on the screened porch, being both indoors and out at the same time, having sun and shade and fresh air, things I'd not felt for months. I couldn't get tired of it, just sitting on the porch and feeling the light breeze come through the bushes around the perimeter of the porch, hearing the wind in the leaves, feeling the warmth of the sun again on the back of my hand. My mother brought lemonade and sandwiches to me. I listened to baseball games on the radio, the familiar deep voice of Jack Brickhouse narrating the comfort-ingly endless story of the adventures of the Chicago Cubs at the end of the season. This is the reason people are baseball fans: Win or lose, home run or strikeout, great catch or bad throw, the game endures forever; you can count on it; you are still there with it. On one side: several books. On the other: my Irish setter, Pat. Bright flowered cushions on white-painted rattan chairs. The pleasures of daily life. Of being alive.

I learned to savor things. I learned, motionless, how to let the world come to me. I learned how to sit for hours and let my mind travel out past the screens into the sunlight, the backyard lawn. This was autumn, the flowers were gone; but the next year and the year after, I would live the whole green season aware of these things as I never had been before, from the fragrance of the lilacs in spring, through the scent of sum-mer roses and freshly mowed grass—so much sweeter now that I didn't have to mow it. Things I had never noticed be-fore. A different world.

These were among the happiest days of my life. These few days, I felt more intensely than most times before or since the great good luck of my flight from death. I saw this life not from the perspective of what I had lost, but from the perspec-tive that I might have lost it all. Whatever else life might hold for me—whether I might recover much of my former self, or only a little of it—I was so grateful for life itself, any bit of it, that any other concern just dropped away. I felt an optimistic anticipation of the future, and I felt complete joy in the pre-sent. It is not often that the three happinesses, of past, present, and future, are all combined in the same moment—and not long before we take it all for granted again.

Thoreau said he had traveled widely in his own back yard. That first weekend home from the hospital, my own travels began even closer to my own body. I noticed the cool leather couch, its smoothness and the fine cracks in its surface; I noticed my own fingerprints. Surely I had noticed them before, but somewhere in myself I understood now that I was remaking myself from the inside out. I was taking inventory. I was noticing what I had and what I didn't have. And my awareness went out in small incremental steps from feeling the skin on my hands, to noticing the smooth desktop of my grandmother's library table, to the different physical qualities of the books near at hand, the sleek dust jacket, the gilt edge, the rough edge—and the slipperiness of magazines in a pile. I lingered on each of these things. They were able to hold my fascination for hours, like a baby's.

I noticed the difference in the quality of the paper in *Better Homes and Gardens* and *Vogue* and *Fortune* and *Time*. Magazines such as *Better Homes and Gardens* are called "dream books" among magazine publishers; they are the magazines that don't pretend to report urgent, useful information; rather, they invite their readers to come and live in a fantasy for a while. I thought all magazines were dream books. *Time*, with its implicit assumption that its readers were busy, powerful men who needed to know succinctly just what they needed to know in order to take charge and run the world, seemed to me a complete dream; I suppose it was especially well suited to that generation of Americans after the Second World War who thought they would make their informed views known to their government, and their government would essentially run the world, accordingly, in a benevolent fashion. Of course,

Fortune was a complete dream magazine; I saw my father, when he read it, feel immediately more powerful and prosperous, reassured, and able to go on with his week.

When I walked through the living room, I felt the fineness of the weave of the Persian carpet through my shoes; it was the perfect walking surface for one on crutches. The foot slid nicely along its nap, the crutch tip sank, reliably anchored, with no danger of slipping, in its firm softness. I am an expert on surfaces. I can tell you, by its footfeel, within a margin of error, roughly how old a given stretch of asphalt road is, just how long ago a hardwood floor was polyurethaned. On the beach, I know, by how far my crutch tip sinks into the sand, about how long ago the tide went out and left the beach to dry. I can tell you just where to walk, along the water line, just the point at which the receding water leaves the sand hardest, so that your crutches won't sink into the sand and make your stroll an ordeal rather than a pleasure.

Loren Eiseley, a naturalist and writer, once wrote of taking a walk in the woods with his dog, and his growing realization, as he was led through the woods from one pleasing sight to another, from colorful wildflowers to dazzling white birch, and as his dog ran excitedly ahead, led from place to place by his nose, that the two of them were taking two entirely different walks in the woods. One lived mostly in a world of sight, the other mostly in a world of scents — two completely different worlds.

I began to feel, like a blind man who comes to rely on his sense of hearing, that I, sitting motionless, must try hard to develop my other senses, to bring the world to me. Of course, everyone comes to this eventually, the need to substitute one human ability for another that has been lost or damaged, to substitute one of the senses for another, to substitute hearing for sight, or sight for hearing, to substitute the mind for the body. It was not something I'd ever had to do until then, but everyone travels this path sooner or later.

By the time my father died in his ninety-fourth year, he had lost most of his hearing and vision. As a young man in Chicago, working for Commonwealth Edison, he had been entitled to free tickets to the Chicago Lyric Opera, and loved it. By the time he was past seventy, his hearing was such that he didn't care much for music. He had always loved golf, and was lucky to play it into his late eighties. Toward the end of his life, his vision was such that he couldn't even follow a game on television. He couldn't read a newspaper, or follow the news on television. He seemed, as the years went on, stupider and stupider, slow in conversation, uncomprehending, ignorant of what was going on around him in the room and in the world. And yet his mind was still as clear and strong and insightful as ever when you connected with him on one subject or another. It was just that he couldn't take in much grist for the mill of his mind, and so he seemed less and less of a person as time went on. So, too, the less physical interaction we have with the world, the less running and jumping and dancing and strolling in the city, so much less is our involvement of all kinds with others, with the things they express in these ways. These losses erode the possible self, and the erosion needs to be worked against with other strategies.

Some things are experienced in one of the senses or another, through sight or touch or hearing; some things are experienced in several of the senses at once. Other things — some of the most complex and exhilarating things — are experienced through the whole body in motion: walking through the woods, playing baseball, dancing, making love. I needed now to discover how to put my whole self in motion in some new way, to find some means of using my mind and my body together to do what previously my body alone had done.

In my bedroom, I turned out the lights in the evening and put on recordings of classical music—music I had never listened to before—and, propping myself against my desk, I stood waving my arms, conducting the orchestra through Beethoven's Fifth, Stravinsky's *Rite of Spring*, Handel and Berg and Schoenberg: flailing through these immense emotions, flying through them in the dark, not feeling in command so much as giving myself over to immense warring, chaotic passions within harmonious, civilized, dependable structures, things that I wanted to feel and to know in my own body.

twelve

Personally, I cried," one boy's father said. "We cried all night long."

"I just couldn't hold up," said the mother of another child. "I don't ever remember crying so hard."

"I feared the boy would be crippled for life, or perhaps in a wheelchair. I mean, you don't want to think about those things because you want to shove them back as far as you can, even though you know he has polio. I think my son can lick it now, because I want to believe that. If I believe otherwise— well, I'm licked myself."

"We tell ourselves, 'My boy, I can see in him possibilities untold. He's quick minded. He's quick on his feet. He's quick with his hands. There's no telling what he'd grow up and do.' . . . It's what we can dream, what we can build in our own minds, our imagination. Polio kills that. It stops that dream. It cuts it short."

"I feel that it will take time, but I feel that he will recover. I strongly feel that he will. . . . I'll say it'll take from two to three months to get him back on his feet completely. I feel that. I don't really know too much about polio."

"It's just that leg, and it's a wonderful thing the work that they do with children now. I feel like Marvin'll walk and he'll walk just as good as he ever did."

"Well, I had to get used to it all over again from what I expected from the beginning. . . . I just thought he was a mild case. And I kind of felt, well, that he would be up and around in at least three months. But I don't expect that now. I think he'll probably be there six months or a year, something like that."

"I don't say that I expected him to be walking around, but I never thought that they'd keep him laying down all the time. It's over two months! . . . I thought he'd at least be sitting in a wheelchair, you know. But I guess if I want him to be well and walking again, I guess that's what he has to go through. . . . It just seems endless, like I'll never see him sitting up."

"Well, I'm waiting for the day when Mr. O. [the physiotherapist] says to me, 'I think he's going to be perfect.' I mean, right now . . . they are not sure. . . . And that's what we're waiting for, when they say he will not need a brace or he will not need a support. I mean that in so-and-so many months he will be a normal child. That's what we're waiting for."

"She really walked awful. . . . it really made me sick because I thought, 'Oh, is that the way she's going to walk?' She could hardly get one leg in front of the other with the brace on. I said, 'Oh, Polly, that's fine, you're just doing fine,' and she was so pleased. And she said, 'Well, I'm going to walk.'"

"I had more hopes. Now I don't know. . . . I mean, it has been, you know, quite a while. And I thought there would be a little improvement . . . But I don't know."

"I'm still looking for improvement, and not exactly what the doctors told me about it taking only a year and a half to two years. The therapy teacher at Norma's school said she knows cases where they don't come along even after the year and a half to two years. And the way she talks, she thought it can happen in four to five years. I pray every night for that."

Parents prayed first, when their children were first stricken with polio, that their children would live. They made promises to God. And after that, they prayed that their children would recover completely.

Just after I got polio, my father started going to church every day before work. He got up at five o'clock in the morning and went to Mass at six. He went to church seven days a week for the next thirty-eight years, until just a few years before he died, when his own frailty made it no longer possible. He never told me why. When I asked him, he was embarrassed; he said he had a promise to keep.

thirteen

After my weekend at home, even though I returned to the hospital my mind was focused on the outside world for good. I understood now that I was not destined to spend years or even months in the hospital. I had been able to negotiate on the outside, however awkwardly, and I now needed only to concentrate hard on my daily exercises, perfect my techniques of standing, balance, walking, the accurate and safe placement of the crutch tip so that it would not hit a slippery spot or loose gravel or a paper clip dropped on a polished floor—and soon I would be home forever.

Like someone who has returned to college in his late twenties or thirties, I knew exactly what I wanted out of my hospital education now, and I got it fast. I got myself into my wheelchair not just once but twice a day to go to sessions with Mrs. Jones; after two weeks, I abandoned the wheelchair permanently and made my way on crutches, on my own, down to the therapy department for Mrs. Jones's coaching. Twice a day I worked to the point of exhaustion, to the moment that my muscles turned to jelly and could not continue. And then I rested until I was ready to go again. I thought of nothing else. I looked on this rebuilding program as training. I learned to walk faster and faster. Often I went down in a clatter of crutches on the hospital floor, and I learned to get back up on my own. I came to feel indestructible—and that was when Mrs. Jones said I was ready to go home to stay.

My mother came at once. There was no drawn-out waiting now. Mrs. Jones said one morning that I could go home. My mother was there by lunchtime. By three o'clock I was gone, back through the trees and rolling hills to home. It was November, the middle of football season, the time of year that always seemed to me the most exhilarating. Autumn has always seemed to me the start of a new year.

To be sure, even though I had come home for good, I needed to go back to the hospital several days a week for an hour or two a day of physical therapy. But from this point on, I don't remember the hospital. I put it completely out of my mind.

Stevie came over the day I got home. We sat on the couch in the living room. She didn't know whether she was meant to be loyal to me still, or not. Just as I had, she had seen movies about veterans returning from World War II. Was she meant to take her hero back, or cut and run and have a normal teenage life?

These things were not mentioned. Neither of us could speak directly, but even young teens know how to come to tacit understandings. She talked about school and friends, the life she had been living while I had been away. I made no suggestion about our seeing each other again. I wanted her to feel free. She never came over again.

We condescend to the feelings of kids, writing them off as the fleeting stuff of a passing phase. But what isn't? As I think back on it, parting with Stevie was as painful as a handful of the most painful things I've felt in life.

A day later, Bets took me to a football game. She had gotten permission to drive right out next to the field, and so we sat in the car and watched the game, with the car windows open to the fresh, bracing November air. I wore a crimson cap with a white B on it—my privileged letter cap from the previous year's time on the football squad.

Girls came over to the car. Boys came over, too, but girls came over to the car: Suzy Harvey, with bright blue eyes, bright red lipstick, a sly smile, a way of staying in constant motion with her body, a readiness for life that couldn't quite be contained. She was put together in the required fashion: short blond hair, a starched white blouse, white angora sweater, a short skirt. Debbie Doolen, whose gaze was direct, inquiring, ready, with no barriers, open and sympathetic to anything she might hear. Remember, this was a fifteen-year-old girl— but she had that capacity for empathy that gives a person understanding way beyond her years. Dark hair, cut short, like Suzy's. She, too, loved sweaters; on that day, she wore a lightweight cardigan with pedal pushers. I'd never noticed the details of my daily life before.

Stevie came over to the car too—undecided, not knowing whether she should behave as a special friend or an old friend or an ex-friend. She put her hand on my arm as it rested on the rolled-down car window, but couldn't look in my eyes, and after a moment let herself be absorbed back into the little crowd. Dave Grinstead. Kinney Smith. And of course my friend Jim, who stayed by the car and talked with me and with Bets for nearly the whole game.

There was a special pleasure not just in being back with my school friends and being at a football game on a beautiful day, but what was even more special was being able to drive the car right out next to the field. This seemed as though it must be a scene from some movie about the returning veteran, the old high school football star being welcomed back after the war. I tried not to play the hero too much, tried to maintain some sense of modesty and humility, in spite of the invitation offered me. But then, as the game went on, I couldn't help noticing that I was now a spectator, and no longer a participant. I was, as the saying goes, on the sidelines. And despite my best efforts to continue to savor the pleasures of heroism, I couldn't resist the growing sensation of being an outsider.

It was as Mrs. Jones had known: Being in the hospital had protected me from understanding what had happened to me. Comparing myself only to the other patients in the hospital, measuring my progress against the progress of those who would never leave the hospital alive, feeling excited with each new step I had been able to take with Mrs. Jones, I had had the feeling I was making an amazing comeback and that each day I could measure some great new piece of progress, with no limits to that progress in sight. Now I saw, all of a sudden, the gulf that separated me from my friends, and from my past life. It turned out that I had lost something. It turned out, for the first time I remember in my life, I missed the past. It turned out that watching the game became increasingly unbearable.

I don't think I felt envy for others. I only felt a sense of loss for myself. But the longer I sat there watching the game, the more I became almost light-headed with the immensity of what I no longer had, of the future I had imagined, counted on, a whole future life that had now been obliterated and that I now needed to forget so that I could go on with some other imagined future. The acts of denial in the hospital—the moments I needed to perform some powerful act of repression so as not to be overwhelmed by fear or sorrow or hopelessness—had to be performed again now. And the pleasure of being at the football game was transformed into a trial of endurance, into a question whether I could stay until the end and continue to the end to look happy in front of my friends.

I became a historian then—that is to say, someone who lived at least in part in his memory, feeling it vividly, able to project myself back into a football game, a locker room, the feel of the padding, the sweat, the showers, the sound of cleats on the locker room floor, the impact of hitting a blocking dummy in practice, of going over and over the story to rewrite it, to see where it went wrong, to know what happened and what it meant. I don't remember having been much interested in the past before I had polio.

At that moment, too, like a historian, I had become riveted by the facts of life, facts that could be so intense as to seem hallucinatory, to bring me to silence. In the quiet and privacy of my bedroom, I was able to review the facts of my own life. There I could take stock of my body in the full-length antique oval mirror that was attached to the dresser that had belonged to my grandmother. From head to toe, from strong jaw to drop foot, I could see what I had to work with; I could note each robust and atrophied muscle, the new, sinuous curvature of my spine, the new smallness of my right buttock, the disappearance of practically all muscle in my left buttock, the compensatory weightlifter's arms and shoulders, good pecs, weak abs, no definition in the stomach muscles, no thighs, no left calf to speak of, an okay right calf, genitals normal and responsive. My right bicep measured eleven and a half inches. My left bicep (less affected by polio) measured twelve and five-eighths. From the low point of 90 pounds after the first weeks in the hospital, I was back to 125, on my way over the next year or so to 140, the greatest share of it in my chest and shoulders and arms. So much of my energy from now on was to be devoted to moving beyond this cluster of facts, negating it, denying its hold on me, reconceiving its meaning, that I needed a reality check in the mirror from time to time, to make certain that whatever else I did I always started with un-denied facts.

The physical concessions that were made to me at home were carefully chosen, enough to help, not enough to get me accustomed to living in any sort of specially constructed world. The parallel bars that I used to get in and out of the house were the only concession in the way of modification to the architecture of my home, and I stopped using them as soon as I could manage the four front steps of brick. There was no special equipment for getting in and out of the bath, nothing special to hold on to except the ordinary banister for going up and down stairs, nothing altered in my bedroom. I learned to accept the world as it was and to adjust to it; that's the way I had been raised.

More recently, as the disability movement got under way, and curbs were changed and entrances made more accessible, I was surprised at how much easier some things became. Changing the world in this way had not occurred to me, and I wasn't sure I liked it. I was in Siena in Italy not long ago, laboring up the steep streets, fearful of slipping on them and falling onto the skull-crushing paving stones, but feeling re-freshed and braced up, too, by meeting the challenge. And in Siena, I noticed, old people who can't make it on the steep streets behind the piazza up toward the duomo are given a helping hand by a nephew or a son or daughter. That seems human. It seems like a good idea for society, personally—not abstractly—to give a hand, a shoulder, to lean on. And yet I'm sure, as I grow older and find myself less and less able to rise to the challenge of such streets, I'll thank the disability movement for having been more civilized and gracious and compassionate than I am.

When I was first at home, I negotiated the stairs up to my bedroom by turning around, sitting down, and going up on my butt. And when my mother asked if she could help by taking my crutches for me, I would say, "No, thanks, I can do it myself." And when she asked if she could help me reach a book or turn on the television or get out of the car or put on a shoe, I would say patiently, "No, thanks," or sometimes I would snap at her that I could do it myself. Hundreds of things were decided in this way, hundreds of ways in which I would be dependent or not, hundreds of ways in which I would adapt to the world as it was.

I felt—Bets felt, I knew—that I needed to defend myself against my mother's instinct to help; and my mother and I survived the strain of that negotiation only because we were so close. Even after she had really absorbed what I needed to do and had begun to try very hard to restrain herself, I had to resist her caring offers more than a dozen times a week. And others offered help too: my father, of course, and friends, and complete strangers. I came to feel embattled against sympathy, which I longed for, feared, sought out, hated, waited for, resented, needed, and rejected. It seemed the enemy to me; this finest and too rare human instinct wanted to keep me in the ghetto of dependency, disabled, limited, unable to do all the things others did, in a category by myself, defining myself by my weaknesses rather than my strengths, by what I couldn't do rather than what I could. I've always refused others' kind offers to let me step ahead of them in a line, preferring to wait my turn like anyone else; I've never had license plates that allow me to park in zones for the disabled. I think these things are good; better-composed people than I would accept them with gratitude. But I've always resisted playing to my weaknesses, for fear it would become a habit and I would begin to think of ever more things I couldn't do, to avoid things that are hard, to take the easy way, give in, give up, be taken care of, be helpless. Sympathy, I thought, could be a mortal threat. And of course pity will just bury you alive. Pity is what we feel for those who are hopelessly inferior to ourselves, who have no chance of recovery, no chance of being human beings with the same inherent value we ourselves have. Someone might have said, some therapist or wise person, Go ahead, let yourself feel it; only then can you grow through it and let it go. But I thought: No. If I let it in, it will bury me; it is too big, I want too much of it, I have an endless hunger for it; if I let down my guard for a moment, I will never surface again. Pity is for victims.

People who have had polio do not like to be called victims, with the attendant implications that they are passive objects to which something has been done, and that their story is over. Rather, they like to think of themselves as active people with more story to live. They like to call themselves survivors, with its hint of having lived through a harrowing experience, tempered for other hard things, maybe even, in some ways, stronger than some others.

I could get dressed by myself now: a wool plaid shirt, khaki trousers, with legs large enough around to accommodate my brace. From time to time, as I sat on the edge of the bed, not quite able to reach down to get the trousers over the brace-encased leg, I would lose my balance and fall to the floor in a heap of metal and textiles.

The brace, which had seemed such a wonderful triumph of outdated technology when I first got it, had come to seem an ugly encumbrance. It did no real good. I couldn't put any weight on my left leg in any case, since the muscles in that hip were too weak to support me, so all the brace did was to keep my knee from constantly buckling even when no weight was put on it. I worked hard to develop the muscles in my left thigh so that even if I could not get my leg strong enough to hold my weight, at least I might develop enough strength to keep the leg straight when I stood up, and leave it to the crutches to bear my weight. I worked attentively at that on my visits to Mrs. Jones, until, just before Christmas, I was able to keep my knee straight and fake walking on my left leg; I took off my leg brace and got around with just my two crutches. To be out of the brace was wonderful; what was even more wonderful was not to have to wear the ugly shoes in which the brace needed to be anchored. I was able to wear the mark of extreme coolness for adolescent boys in the fifties: white bucks. My sister Sookie gave them to me when she came home for Christmas.

Now I found myself practicing standing, not just standing so I wouldn't fall over, but standing like someone who is cool, whose body has natural grace. Of course, since my body didn't have natural grace, I overcompensated: I stood too nicely. I stood like a ballet dancer waiting in the wings after a performance to see if anyone intends to compliment him. My aesthetic was way off.

According to the Oxford English Dictionary, to be beautiful is to be "attractive or impressive through expressing or suggesting fitness, order, regularity, rhythm, cogency, or perfection of structure." A whole organism, as the physician Eric Cassell has written, "is not whole in merely the biological sense." Every life, as Cassell says, has a sense of wholeness or correctness, of fitness and cogency, that is made up of the remembered common past of the family, of the web of friendships and relationships, of expectations and hopes for the future that inform the present, of the unconscious dreams and fears, of the continuously rewritten autobiography we all carry with us in our minds; and all of these are subject to damage. The loss of an expected future, the location for hope, can be shattering. Illness damages our aesthetic sense of our lives— and that is a source of suffering as much as any physical pain. The aesthetic whole of a life must be reconstructed if a person is to regain a sense of coherence.

Sookie knew this without ever reading Eric Cassell. She got me a Scotch plaid beret, and then a red vest, and then gray flannel trousers, a plaid bow tie, a rep stripe silk tie, a handkerchief for my jacket pocket. While I was rebuilding from the inside out, she rebuilt from the outside in.

Or not rebuilt, but built almost from scratch: What was wanted was a new person, because the old one would never be restored. Somehow, at this time, I found I could no longer avoid the knowledge that I suppose I must have absorbed the moment Mrs. Jones said I could leave the hospital: I was released because not much more could be done for me. With a sudden shock, I realized she had abandoned me. To be sure, she had done it gently. She had sent me on into the world with her affection and support, telling me—to ease the separation—that I must continue to come back to the hospital from time to time for therapy; but she meant that from now on, I must make my own way. And I must not expect much more improvement in my physical progress.

These bits of news—that really I would never go back onto a football field, that really I had reached a plateau of recovery, that really I was to be crippled the rest of my life—I had managed to space out the recognition of this news over some period of months. But their cumulative weight bore down on me now so that I felt a dull ache of despair. More and more, it was an effort to get up each day and raise my spirits high enough again to carry on. Each day I had to talk to myself, to negotiate with the boy who wanted to call it quits, give up, grow bitter, be cynical, withdraw, lash out; to wreck what was not already wrecked so that all that was around him would correspond to some inner truth of his life. Each day I had to say to that boy, You're still alive, you're lucky, you have a loving family, good friends; what did you think, that life would be a free ride? You're not so bad off; have some sense of perspective. Look at all you still can do. Use your anger to fuel some ambition; you have privileges and comforts and possible futures that millions of others would give an arm and a leg for.

Most of this psychological warfare I conducted on my own. As Josephine Walker, who got polio some years before I did, wrote, "nobody discussed it. . . . My parents did everything for me that was needed physically. . . . They were in total denial about the fact that there was an emotional component to this. And so they pretended, after a while, like it didn't happen, other than the fact that I needed—you know—a little bit of medical help. People didn't talk about the implications of it for my life. They just kind of let me go."

Polio survivors and their families had three basic strategies they could choose among or combine in some fashion in welcoming a child on crutches or in a wheelchair back home from the hospital and helping him to reconceive his identity.

The least preferred strategy was a frank avowal of the truth: that the child being brought home was different from other children. But this acknowledgment of difference, while it might certainly have been on everyone's unconscious mind, was unbearable for most families, since to be different inevitably meant to be inferior. The child who accepted the stigma of being "not like other children" very often found himself on the road to withdrawal from the society of normals, to isolation, and, in time, to bitterness and anger and self-hatred.

A much preferred strategy, according to Fred Davis, was "passing," or the outright denial that a child was "different," or even that she had had polio at all. That was a plausible strategy if the results of the polio were not too obvious, or if they could be covered up. One boy, recently out of the hospital and wearing a cast on his leg, was riding with his parents in a taxi. The driver asked, "How'd you break your leg, son? Playing football?" And his mother hastened to reply that was exactly what had happened. When they got out of the cab, the boy said to his mother, "Am I glad you didn't tell him I had polio! He just thinks I have a broken leg." Among the preferred passing personae: the injured athlete, the veteran of a foreign war, the avid skier.

As good as passing was, however, some people couldn't pass all the time, or under all circumstances, and so they needed to choose carefully those occasions when they could get away with passing, which requires constant attentiveness, resorting to a supplementary third strategy for everyday use. That strategy was what Davis has called "normalization," which, without going to the extent of denying the existence of a physical handicap outright, would nonetheless sustain the " 'democratic' fiction that the impairment was of no consequence in social relations and that the child was, for all practical purposes, 'normal, like everyone else.' "

The egalitarian American family was especially well suited to this strategy, since such families had already adopted the easygoing, anti-elitist attitude that it didn't matter if one child was taller than another, or faster or smarter or more athletic.

Of all these strategies, normalization was the hands-down favorite. "Other things being equal," as Davis says, "this is perhaps to be expected in view of our society's pronounced idealization of the normal, the healthy, the physically attractive. . . . as a people we are suspicious of most forms of eccentricity; we tend to recoil from manifestations that depart from a relatively narrow social definition of 'the normal,' be they of a moral, characterological, or physical bent. Hence . . . families found it [easy] to assimilate the social deviance latent in the child's handicap to the cultural framework of 'normal' aspirations and imagery already internalized by them."

In truth, I'm not sure anyone was able to bring off any one of these strategies in its pure theoretical form. In my own family, anyway, I would say we aspired to normalization in combination with opportunistic passing accompanied by the occasional necessary quick embarrassed recognition of the truth.

For our first Thanksgiving dinner after I had returned from the hospital, my mother gathered the family around for a wonderfully normalizing day. My glamorous Aunt Douga flew to Barrington to be with us, and my cousins Betty and Casey, both in their twenties at that time, also came for the weekend: the extended family rallied to give tacit support and thanks for my homecoming (all but Sookie, who was completely taken up with being a college girl in Colorado). In the living room after dinner, everyone arrayed themselves in a tableau attesting to the faith that, whatever damage the family had sustained, life would go on for many more years, comfortable, secure, and on a normal course. Casey, tall and demure in a tweed suit, with a modest gaze; her sister Betty, wide-eyed and sexy; Aunt Douga, the dazzling New Yorker in basic black with a single strand of pearls and fire-engine-red lipstick; my own sister Bets, with her silver locket around her neck; my mother, with large pearl earrings and a beige cardigan sweater; my father, in his casual holiday dress—gray flannel trousers, hand-knit argyle socks, a red and green plaid Pendleton shirt—standing with easy confidence, holding a china cup and saucer in his hand; my Irish setter, Pat, stretched out on the carpet, elegant and soulful; even I myself, stretched out on the leather couch, wearing a navy blue pullover: all gave testimony by their warm, relaxed, slightly worn and tired, happy presence that the family was intact and so were its members.

And yet, even as I appreciated this sense of returning and belonging to my family, and its warm instinct to bring me back as one who could almost pass, I felt myself no longer quite in my family, quite able to continue its strategies of getting on in the world, its ways of seeing the world and living. To my sorrow, the stories the family told itself seemed just a little false to me now, and distant.

Aunt Douga, that Thanksgiving, asked me question after

question about my polio—questions so curious and direct and enthusiastic that my mother and father were made silent and anxious in the background, afraid that talking about polio would upset me. I responded to her questions eagerly—glad, finally, to be able to talk about the forbidden subject, but also still uncertain and confused about what the experience had been, what it meant, how I felt about it. Aunt Douga, who had written a few books of her own, concluded her interrogation with the happy and firm conviction that I should write a book about it. The moment she said so, I was crushed and shut up. The last thing I wanted to do was to become a poster boy, to turn my story into something maudlin and humiliating. Aunt Douga saw how I recoiled from her suggestion. She asked if I had heard of Samuel Johnson. I hadn't. She told me about him, the great dictionary he had written, and his chronic, lifelong depression. Johnson, she said, had once declared that every book has a moral purpose, and that purpose is to give others the courage to go on.

But I couldn't begin to grasp what she was saying. I hadn't come through this experience yet; I was still stuck in the middle of it, the helpless victim of regret and confusion and false good cheer. The moment my aunt suggested I write such a book, I was overcome by a sense of my lack of robustness, my feebleness of spirit, my inner complaints, the character traits of a loser that had taken possession of me. She was expecting some sort of brave and inspiring movie or television comeback, and for not having made such a comeback—indeed, for having poured scorn on the very idea of such a comeback—I felt ashamed. Far from being able to give others the courage to go on, I didn't have the courage myself. And the world to which

I was meant to return seemed every day more and more remote.

I was not yet quite quick enough on my crutches to navigate going back to school, but Bets began bringing home my schoolbooks for me, and I started to catch up with the work I'd missed. In truth, since I didn't need to spend a lot of time goofing off in class, I got through my schoolwork in short order, and I spent many hours in the living room, watching Ed Sullivan's *Toast of the Town* and Sid Caesar's *Your Show of Shows* and *Ozzie and Harriet* and *I Love Lucy*.

These shows, and their commercials, made me dizzy with their vision of a world so wholesome, intact, healthy, vigorous, upbeat, smooth-skinned, smiling, sleek, plump; with all the unattainable girls in swimming suits, each one of them incredibly sexy even as they were evidently not thinking about sex or anything other than purity, purity of soap and purity of complexion and purity of thought, the purity of a perfect Ipana toothpaste smile; clean people, good people, winning people, with their milk shakes and hamburgers and French fries, bobby sox and swirling skirts and snug sweaters, their pep and vigor. This world seemed so foreign to me, and at the same time so familiar: actually, in many confusing ways, this vision of the close-knit, happy family, secure in the possession of the basic consumer durables, described my life. But at the same time, in some way I couldn't put my finger on, I knew this was not my world at all. I thought: Oh, I think I know how *Negroes* feel. I thought: These people on television could be from the *moon*.

fourteen

Disneyland opened in July 1955, its inaugural ceremonies broadcast on television, hosted by Bob Cummings, Art Linkletter, and Ronald Reagan. "I think," Cummings said, "that everyone here will one day be as proud to have been at *this* opening as the people who were there at the dedication of the Eiffel Tower!" Fess Parker, who starred as Davy Crockett in the weekly Disney television series, was there, and Cinderella and Roy Rogers and Dale Evans and Sleeping Beauty, Frank Sinatra, Debbie Reynolds, Donald Duck, and Walt Disney himself. Disneyland dissolved reality. The departure from any facts of life, even easy, agreeable facts of life, was complete: there were not even any suburbs here in Tomorrowland and Frontierland and Adventureland and Fantasyland.

The center of Disneyland was Main Street USA, circa 1900, the quintessence of order, uniformity, perkiness, friendliness. It was sunny, easygoing, and perfect. Even normality itself was made just a little more accommodating and ingratiating here: every window and doorway on the ground floor of the shops on Main Street was made seven-eighths its true size. The second story of each building was five-eighths scale (as were the trains and boats of Disneyland), the top stories one-half. This was a diminutive human scale so neighborly and intimate as to be adorable. It was, said the architect Charles Moore, "a musical comedy village."

All the shops on Main Street sold things, mainly Mickey Mouse memorabilia. Its very lovableness caused strollers to relax and forget their sales resistance—as Disneyland's planners had planned: "Actually," as one of them said, "what we're selling is reassurance."

Within the first few hours it was open, more than thirty thousand people were drifting through Disneyland, with many millions more to follow. They couldn't have got there without the family car. The standard car of the times, as Karal Ann Marling has written in her book about life in the fifties, *As Seen on TV,* was the family car—not the personal car like the British or Italian sports car, but the family car, suitable for Dad taking Mom and the kids on an outing. To be sure, this car was a luscious, baroque thing, like a piece of eighteenth-century French architectural pastry, with its smooth, plump fenders, its streaks and splashes and encrustations of chrome, the gratuitous chrome-framed double headlights and the huge chrome bumpers and grills like sharks' teeth on the front, the lubricious flourishes of tailfin at the rear, dashboards splattered with chrome knobs and buttons and dials, and clocks with green glow-in-the-dark hands. It was equipped with Dynaflow transmission and power windows and power brakes, wraparound windshields, and AM radios. All this just to take Mom to the supermarket, Dad to the golf course, and the kids to the swimming pool. Elvis had three Cadillacs by 1956, one in bright yellow, one in black and pink to match his wardrobe, and one classy white El Dorado with white sidewall tires and creamy leather upholstery.

The family car transformed America, moving the middle

class to the suburbs, to backyard barbecues and next-door neighbors, lawns and television sets and washers and dryers, the one-family house, the car in the driveway, and on the railroad station platform, commuting to their jobs in the city, white men in hats.

As I look at photographs from that time, it seems I had once fit easily into this world: a crew-cut boy with a big toothy smile, coming into the age when he is allowed to sit in the stern and command the outboard motorboat on the summer lake; a boy in a tweed jacket, with his arm protectively around his grandmother who is now an inch or two shorter than he is; a boy in a plaid shirt, with his father and a brace of ducks they have shot together; a boy helping his father bring in the Christmas tree; a boy with his father, standing on the first tee, before a round of golf.

This world was not as comfortable with deviance as it was with painting by numbers. As the ads said: "Another adventure of the Ozzie Nelsons . . . they paint original Picture Craft oil paintings. Yes . . . families everywhere are painting original Picture Craft! Just like the Ozzie Nelsons . . . you, too, will prefer original Picture Craft. An exclusive process enables you to re-create a true work of art. It's fun, relaxing, you need no experience—and it's GUARANTEED!" Each kit included an instruction manual, a "special artist's brush," tubes of pre-mixed artist's colors, and a canvas 12 by 16 inches with little coloring-book shapes, each numbered to correspond to one of the numbered tubes of paint so that when the numbered colors were daubed inside the lines of the numbered shapes, out came a dog, or Leonardo da Vinci's *Last Supper* or a New England landscape. A masterpiece. Paint-by-numbers took off that autumn I came home from the hospital; it was the hottest gift of Christmas 1953. President Eisenhower gave paint-by-numbers sets to members of the White House staff. It was even something you could do while you watched television.

What's to be said of this? A new standard for conformity? Really, like the Grand Canyon or Mozart, painting by numbers begs for a respectful silence in the face of an awesome fact. It transcends commentary. An epoch that celebrated painting by numbers was an epoch whose values and preferences and standards of desirability were beyond argument. I myself was given a kit to paint by numbers.

And for those who couldn't make the pilgrimage all the way to California, Disneyland came into their homes every week on television, with stories of Davy Crockett, cowboys taking the West with decency, fairness, toughness: good winners and happy families.

In the TV sitcoms of the day, there were no poor families, no black families, no broken families, no jobless families, no families in which there was any serious sickness, especially no mental illness, and no problem so difficult that it could not be resolved before the final commercial break. Mothers and fathers liked each other, and their children liked them, and the worst thing any father did was to be a bit of a doofus, which the whole family found endearing.

No one knew in exactly what state or what suburb the sitcom families lived; they lived in a land of nostalgia for early, simple America. Even my own mother, who always seemed to me someone who never lost her grip on the essentials of life, who always understood what was to be valued and treasured, who always stood outside the fads of the day, even my own mother had two of the chairs in the living room reupholstered in an "early American" fabric and, for one of the end tables, got a lamp in the style of a kerosene lantern of the frontier; and my father had a real little gas lamp installed just outside the front door for a porch light.

Nonetheless, the fifties did not go so far in my own home as to invade the kitchen, and so I didn't entirely recognize the pictures of the RCA Whirlpool "miracle" kitchen run by an electronic brain that was put together for an American exhibition in Moscow in 1959. The kitchen had sleek, uncluttered counters and eye-level shelves for dishes and spices and an automated "Mechanical Maid" that cleaned the floor and put itself away. Altogether, the kitchen proved to the Russians what it was meant to prove: that American capitalism was superior to Russian Communism, that the Russians were pathetic losers, stuck in their deviant economic system while the West went from robust victory to exultant triumph. The pavilion in which the exhibition was housed, writes Marling, contained a rack of more than 5,000 "pots and pans, dishes, rolling pins, and small appliances . . . showcased like so many precious jewels: spectators could see the items from a special viewing balcony, but they remained just out of reach." The Russians forbade Coty to distribute free lipsticks to Russian women, or to allow Helena Rubinstein's model beauty salon to give free makeovers. But free glasses of Pepsi were given away at the rate of 10,000 an hour for the 1,008 hours of the exhibition, where the Russians were also treated to a display of hi-fi sets, cigarettes, sewing machines, refrigerators, houses, groceries, twenty-two new American cars, stoves, lounge chairs, and breakfast cereal; furthermore, according to Marling, "the rituals of American family life, from the wedding and the honeymoon to the backyard barbecue and the country club dance, were enacted four times daily by fashion models in typical American outfits."

In one of the model American kitchens, Soviet premier Nikita Khrushchev and U.S. vice president Richard Nixon engaged in a debate of stupefying banality that was, at the same time, in the very dadaism of it, quintessentially Fifties Cold War. The two men, touring the exhibition together with a gaggle of reporters and television cameramen following them, began to bicker with each other when Nixon bragged about a display of television sets, and Khrushchev dismissed his enthusiasm, saying, "In another seven years we will be on the same level as America. When we catch you up, in passing you by, we will wave to you." Nixon was stung by the retort, and then, a little while later, when they paused in front of one of the model kitchens at the exhibition, Nixon said, "I want to show you this kitchen. It is like those of our houses in California."

"We have such things," said Khrushchev, unimpressed.

But, said Nixon, anyone can afford this kitchen and the $14,000 house that goes with it. On a mortgage running twenty-five to thirty years, a steelworker, for instance, would only have to pay $100 a month.

Khrushchev was contemptuous. The house wouldn't be standing that long, he said. "We build firmly. We build for our children and grandchildren." The Russians were not impressed by all this glittering American trivia.

"We hope to show our diversity and our right to choose," said Nixon. "We do not want our decisions made at the top by one government official that all houses should be the same. . . . Let the people choose the kind of house . . . the kind of ideas they want."

That was the end of the debate.

Khrushchev's idea about the good life was inexplicably just, well, "different." And the Russians were just pitiable rubes, or would have been had they not had the atomic bomb. The bomb hung over the fifties in a way difficult to imagine these days. When the bomb was first tested in Alamogordo, George Kistiakowsky, one of its developers, said: "In the last milli-second of the earth's existence, the last men will see what we saw." When J. Robert Oppenheimer returned to his office, he found a young researcher outside the building vomiting. When Albert Einstein was asked with what weapons World War III would be fought, he replied that he didn't know, but he knew the next war after World War III would be fought with rocks.

This dread was all-pervasive in the fifties. It seeped into every crevice of life; it poisoned politics; it invited anxiety in private life; it may account for some of the dadaism in the world of entertainment.

I missed the telecast of the full kitchen debate, but, as I was recuperating at home, I did spend a good deal of time in front of a television set during the last days of the career of Senator Joseph McCarthy, who might have gone on forever building a successful career by finding Communists lurking in the corners of the American government, who were infiltrating the system like viruses, a contagion threatening to bring America to its knees, had he not made the mistake of alleging that Communists had worked their way into the United States Army. The Army fought back, and I watched almost the whole of the Army–McCarthy hearings as I recuperated at home in the living room. But even then, despite the defeat of

McCarthy at the hands of the U.S. Army, anticommunism continued to flourish.

Goodness had won World War II—goodness and egalitarian forthrightness. The decent GIs, the gals back home who waited for them, we fought hard, we fought clean, we didn't torture anyone or do anything sneaky. We had nothing to hide. We were what we seemed, and proud of it: strong, whole, well-groomed, clean-shaven, robust, vigorous, can-do, optimistic. Really, with an understandable love of victorious America and all it had stood for during the recent war, and with the new postwar anticommunism as the irreducible core, the culture turned against deviance of all kinds, was suspicious of it, and, it might be, even hated it.

I felt I had to take this personally. If everyone was celebrating the idea of the normal, the healthy, the robust can-do life, then my chances for prospering, or maybe even surviving, were in danger. Only if the boundaries of the normal were extended, or if the abnormal were enthusiastically embraced, did I have a chance to survive, let alone prosper.

It may be that this hostility toward difference was not merely a manifestation of McCarthy or of the fifties or even of America, but the manifestation of a more deep-seated human urge. Just as a baby knows who it is by knowing who it is not, just as a word is defined by saying what it does not mean and what it does not include, so a society defines itself by saying what it is not and what it does not include. A society must do this, just as a baby must, in order to have a coherent life. At the same time, if a society is too strict about this, it will stop evolving and die. It's the job of the deviants to extend the boundaries of what it is to be an acceptable person. The presence of deviants forces the society to be more encompassing, to take in a larger view of what it is to be human, to become more humane. This is a never-ending struggle, to make a society that coheres but that is humane and vital. This is the continuing work of all civilizations forever. But, in the fifties, in Barrington, there did seem to be a terrible shortage of deviants.

Meanwhile, I needed to fight my way through the false narratives that were offered to me, consciously or not, by my family's world—and at the same time, even as I recognized the falseness of the stories, say, of willpower, I didn't want to dismiss them entirely, because I also needed every bit of my will. I knew the stories of fighting and of heroism were puffed-up entertainment for other people, but I knew, too, that I could help myself along if I bought in to them a little bit.

And I also knew it was no good to drop into cynicism about all these things that kept appearing on television and in the magazines. Cynicism, as I kept telling myself, was useless and time consuming, and I had more serious things to do. If I did feel resentment, I needed to repress it. It was not constructive. I had to avoid distractions, the indulging of emotions that would lead me to dead ends. I needed to find something that was real and true and constructive. But what was real and true? My thoughts and feelings, like my recovering muscles, were in constant flux. My job was to bring them, like my odd musculature, toward some useful, harmonious balance to sustain myself, please others, secure myself some space and permission to carry on as only I knew best, to get people to stand back and to support me at the same time. Yet I had to be careful not to construct a completely false persona that would make me lose touch with my true self, the self that really sustained me. I couldn't let my feelings overwhelm me, and at the same time I couldn't let myself become ice cold, because that would not do, either; it was not pleasing to others or fun for me. While I was managing my emotions, I also needed to make some effort at spontaneity, true spontaneity, because people like that, and because it is what a real human being is, and I wanted to be a real human being, not a false one, not a damaged one, not a partial or limited one. I needed to learn how to feel my real feelings without letting them swamp and drown me—until I finally got to a place where I actually felt optimistic feelings and didn't need to fake them any more.

During all this time, my mother took me everywhere, back to the hospital for physical therapy three times a week, and, once a week, to the neighboring town of Glencoe, where some good person had given over his heated swimming pool in the winter to those with all sorts of disabilities. The first time we went, I was apprehensive. I had loved the hot whirlpool baths at the hospital, but I feared I might drown in a deep swimming pool. I was lowered into the pool by two men, and I clung to the edge of the deep end for several minutes until I gradually realized that, because I had lost so much weight to polio and the air in my lungs had less mass to keep afloat, I was as buoyant as a corked bottle. I let go of the side of the pool and floated out into the warm water, free at last of every tug of gravity that had rendered me weak and clumsy. In the water, I moved with grace and, because of the new strength of my arms, with speed. I moved like a porpoise. I could turn somersaults in the water. I could lie on my back, put my hands behind my head, and float forever; I could have napped if I'd wanted. I could go underwater, twisting and turning somersaults, rise to the surface, submerge again, turning over and over, until I was dizzy, no longer knowing up from down but trusting my body to rise to the air when it needed to, my body back in touch with the physical world in a completely thoughtless way, taking care of itself and of me as it used to do.

It was on these drives to and from Glencoe, when my mother and I were alone, in quiet and intimate conversation as we passed through the countryside, that we became closer than we had ever been before. My mother's entire life was taken up with her family. She had no other life and, I think, wanted no other life. Her own mother had been a woman who might have run a country—and had run a large farm. Her sister had gone to New York to make a dazzling career as a radio star. She herself had started out on a career in business, and in photographs of her in the 1920s when she was herself in her twenties, she looks like a hot young woman, a flapper, fully capable of a glamorous and independent life in New York or Paris. But she came to marriage and family as her calling and gave herself to her family completely—to a fault, I would say; vanished into her family, I would say. All her children wished she would be more assertive, live *her* life. But I think she did; her life was giving herself to her family, to the continuing life of the family, which she believed was the continuing life of civilization itself. And so, although she would riffle through the pages of *Vogue* from time to time, although she had elegant taste and from time to time would buy a suit that was in keeping with the "New Look" of the fifties ("We were leaving a period of war," Christian Dior said, "of uniforms, of soldier-women with shoulders like boxers. I turned them into flowers, with soft shoulders, blooming bosoms, waists slim as vine stems, and skirts opening up like blossoms"), she was not much taken with fashion or with what fashionable people held to be valuable or worthwhile. She practiced the virtues of civilization: good listening, careful and considerate speech, generosity, compassion, supportiveness, honesty, warmth. She took these as her vocation and hoped her family would go out whole into the world to practice her example.

My mother revealed her anger about my polio just once; in fact, it was the only time in my entire life that I ever saw her angry. We were driving back from Glencoe one day after I had been swimming, and we stopped at a railroad crossing. A pickup truck behind us tapped us gently on the rear bumper. My mother flushed with anger. Trembling with rage, she put the gearshift into Park and got out of the car and walked back to the truck that had bumped us—and she screamed at the driver, screamed and screamed and screamed at him.

fifteen

█ first heard of Jonas Salk and his polio vaccine that fall when I got home from the hospital. I hadn't known anyone had been working on a vaccine, though of course a lot of other people knew about it.

Jonas Salk, the eldest son of Russian Jewish immigrants, was born in 1914 and attended medical school at New York University. Immigrant's son, poor boy, Jew, outsider: luckily, just as he finished his internship at Mount Sinai, one of his professors from NYU had been appointed the director of the new School of Public Health at the University of Michigan. Salk followed his professor, Dr. Thomas Francis, Jr., to Ann Arbor. Francis was working to find a vaccine against influenza. As it happened, the U.S. military was urgently interested in supporting that effort: 6 million people had died in the flu epidemic that broke out in the turmoil at the end of World War I. More American soldiers had died of the flu than had died in combat, and the Army was eager to avoid a repetition.

And so, from 1942 to 1947, Salk worked under Thomas Francis on developing a flu vaccine—and then, hoping to get out on his own, hoping to become a "principal investigator," he finally landed a job at the University of Pittsburgh, which was not, at that time, one of the more prestigious medical schools; Salk's Virus Research Lab there was not even one of its more distinguished or better-funded departments. Looking for grants to sustain his lab, Salk signed up for a virus-typing project sponsored by the National Foundation for Infantile Paralysis. The project was simply a research program to find out exactly how many types of polio virus there were. It was thought there might be as many as 196 different viruses — which would make the development of a vaccine immensely complicated. Salk worked for three years, and used 17,500 laboratory monkeys in his tests for the polio viruses. In 1951, he announced that there were just three viruses.

Salk had thought of his research on virus-typing as dull, plodding work, but it gave his lab a dependable income — which Salk thought would support him while he pursued his more interesting influenza research. But of course the virus-typing led Salk gradually into other areas of research on polio.

As it happened, in the same year that Salk went to the Virus Research Lab, three Harvard medical researchers, Dr. John Enders and his young associates Thomas H. Weller and Frederick C. Robbins, succeeded for the first time in growing polio virus outside the body. Before that, in order to get a quantity of virus for research it had been necessary to infect monkeys with the virus, care for them until they were just at the right stage of illness, and then kill them to grind up their spinal columns and recover the live virus from the mess.

Everyone engaged in polio research understood that Enders's discovery was extraordinary news: the production of large quantities of the virus would make research that much easier and faster—and eventually might provide the means to produce enough virus to manufacture a polio vaccine. Only Salk, however, took advantage of the news by equipping his lab immediately to produce the virus as Enders had shown.

The principle of a vaccine is to inject a person with a form of the virus potent enough to provoke an antibody response, but not so strong as to cause an infection. The vaccine can be made from a virus that has been killed so that it can no longer proliferate, or a live virus that has been so weakened, the infection it causes is mild enough to be harmless. For the dead-virus vaccine, the virus is killed by being heated or treated with chemicals, most often formaldehyde. Live-virus vaccines are weakened by having the virus passed from one laboratory animal to another laboratory animal, or from culture medium to culture medium, until it is sufficiently attenuated. The live-virus vaccine does carry a statistically extremely small risk of actually causing an infection—as the dead-virus vaccine does not—but the champions of the live-virus vaccine argued that it was the most natural method and that it was longer-lasting. Indeed, in the short history of vaccinations to that date, there was no evidence that a dead-virus vaccine would provide protection for more than a few months.

Among the other medical researchers working on a polio vaccine, one who was widely respected by his peers, was Dr. Albert Sabin. He believed that the attenuated live virus was the preferred basis for a vaccine.

Nonetheless, in Salk's view, a few months' protection might carry hundreds of thousands of children safely through the polio season. He was interested in fast results—as was his sponsor, the National Foundation. And then, too, Salk had worked with a killed virus in his research on the flu vaccine, so he felt comfortable taking what he knew into this related field.

John Enders objected to Salk's work, saying that the widespread use of a killed-virus vaccine might so disrupt the natural epidemiology of the disease that it would make the population as a whole even more vulnerable to polio. Dr. Sabin said the killed-virus vaccine would be a pernicious distraction—an investment of time and money and public support in a temporary measure instead of mobilizing all those resources for the lasting solution that a live-virus vaccine would provide.

Others had other objections to Salk. He was pushy. He was "ambitious," that is to say, in the euphemism of the time: Jewish. He had already acquired a reputation while he was working in Thomas Francis's lab of wanting to rush a scholarly paper into print—and take credit for a discovery—before Francis thought the hypothesis was quite proven. Salk was not, after all, one of the distinguished scientists in the field of polio research, not really a member of the club, having been a mere applied scientist in the field of influenza vaccine. He was becoming a little too much the pet researcher of the National Foundation, whose showbiz fund-raising tactics did not seem, to most researchers, compatible with the quiet and patience necessary for good, trustworthy science. As one doctor said, Salk's work habits resembled the way he had once been seen driving up one of Pittsburgh's cobble streets after an icy winter storm: "He was going up, no matter what, and the way he was going up was, he'd drive his car, and his car would swing into the curb, and he'd swing out and start back up. I don't know what he did to the car, but he was determined to get up.

He had things to do, and he did. Other people were stuck down there."

When Salk had found himself sailing to a polio conference in Copenhagen in 1951, Sabin was on board the same ship, and, as Salk recalled it, "Albert came and put his arm around me and talked about establishing a polio research institute. How great it would be to have Joe Melnick [another researcher] and me with him, Melnick being the other 'bright young man' in polio work. We'd have meetings every morning and we'd decide what to do and what not to do. One big happy family. I was rather laconic about it, I suppose. I was busy laying plans for my own work, and the prospect of submitting to Albert in a kind of institutionalized typing-committee arrangement was not what I had in mind for myself. He really is a remarkable fellow. During the voyage . . . it became obvious to anyone who had not heard of it before that I was a nice young whippersnapper from Pittsburgh, going to Denmark to report on some drudgery I had performed. I might have failed abysmally, it seemed clear, if Albert had not been up in the flies, pulling the strings and setting the standards."

As Jews, both Sabin and Salk were regarded as outsiders in the community of American medical scientists. (Sabin, it was said, was "white-haired, dark-eyed, with a sharp nose, small dark moustache, nubbin chin, and general mien of Reynard the Fox" with an unctuous manner and "a resemblance on occasions to Groucho Marx.") But Sabin had already had a long and distinguished career in the scientific community, whereas Salk was seen as an unpolished newcomer, even by Sabin.

However, Salk had found a compatible friend in Basil O'Connor, head of the National Foundation, the son of a tinsmith, the child of a Boston family of refugees from the Irish potato famines—"two generations removed from servitude," as he enjoyed saying—a man who had worked his way up to be, by the age of thirty-five, the proprietor of private railway cars, limousines, and a gentleman's farm in Long Island, and to be a law partner of Franklin Roosevelt.

By 1950, Salk was eager to take his killed-virus vaccine, which he had tried to good effect on monkeys, and test it on some children. As he wrote to Dr. Harry Weaver, the director of research at the National Foundation, he had found "that not too far from here there are institutions for Hydrocephalics and other similar unfortunates. I think that we may be able to obtain permission for a study of immunization [on them]. . . . I think we might be able to transfer patients to the Municipal Hospital, keeping them under isolation." The children, wards of the state, would be taken away from their familiar surroundings, isolated in Pittsburgh's Municipal Hospital, injected with his experimental vaccine, and then exposed to a live polio virus. Salk thought something might be done, too, with "inmates of prisons who might volunteer for such studies." (!)

Weaver turned him down. But two years later, after more work on the vaccine, after Salk had tried it on himself, on members of his lab, and on his own children, he was given permission to try his vaccine on residents of the Polk State School for retarded male children and adults near Pittsburgh. He gave lollipops to the one hundred inmates who participated in the test on May 23, 1952. Nobody got sick.

On June 12, 1952, he tried his vaccine on forty-five children at the D. T. Watson Home for Crippled Children. To set a good example, and to share the risk, twenty-seven staff members of the Watson Home also volunteered to take the

vaccination. "When you inoculate children with a polio vaccine," Salk said, "you don't sleep well for two or three
months." But nobody got sick. Returning to the Home again
and again during the summer, Salk took blood samples: Antibody levels had risen, and stayed up. The vaccine worked.

Salk reported his results at a meeting of polio researchers
convened by the National Foundation in Hershey, Pennsylvania, on January 24, 1953. Sabin immediately declared that
years of additional study would be needed before one could
say Salk had a usable, or even a testable, vaccine. Vaccinations
given to cripples at the Watson Home could hardly be considered anything other than boosters to the immunity they
had already acquired by having had polio. Sabin proposed another ten to fifteen years of research to find a proper level of
killed-virus vaccine suitable for testing. No doubt jealousy
played a part in Sabin's remarks; but his position also repre-
sented the more respectable, and prudent, scientific opinion.
Many of those who supported Sabin feared that a hasty attempt to vaccinate thousands of children might itself set loose
a horrifying epidemic of fatal disease.

Salk was eager to proceed with more testing, with a big
field trial—and with distribution of the vaccine around the
country. Basil O'Connor was also eager to launch a vaccine.
At one meeting of medical researchers, as one of the meeting's
participants recalled, "O'Connor sat there writing figures on a
yellow pad and listening to the scientists go around in circles"
about whether or not a safe vaccine would be ready to test
soon. "Suddenly he said, 'I have just figured out that during
this coming summer thirty or forty thousand children will get
polio. About fifteen thousand of them will be paralyzed and
more than a thousand will die. If we have the capacity to pre-

vent this, we have a social responsibility. . . . it is our duty to save lives, no matter how many difficulties may be involved."

Two days after the meeting at Hershey, Dr. Harry Weaver briefed the board of the National Foundation on Salk's research. The next day, newspapers all over the world reported that there was a new polio vaccine. On February 9, *Time* magazine welcomed the news of Salk's vaccine and said it would probably be available in time for a large-scale field test later that year. This little flurry of media coverage hardly helped Salk's reputation with his fellow scientists, who continued to murmur that he was a publicity seeker and glory hound.

The millions of Americans who had contributed dimes to the National Foundation for the past decade and more were suddenly in a swivel to get their hands on the vaccine. And so Salk compounded his bad reputation with the scientific community. In the middle of March, Salk offered to go on the CBS radio network to address the nation and put things in perspective for anxious parents. He spoke at some length, starting with the history of the disease, of the discovery in 1909 that it was a viral disease. He sounded like the very paragon of the caring physician, healer, scientist. He spoke deliberately, patiently. He explained what he believed his vaccine could do — that it could provide protection against polio for a short term, for the length of a polio season; but it was not yet ready. "Certain things cannot be hastened," he said. More work needed to be done before he could distribute the vaccine with confidence. He sounded the very quintessence of scientific prudence, even as he rushed to get his vaccine ready to test.

And still, his fellow scientists argued against him fiercely. In June of 1953, Albert Sabin addressed the American Medical

Association: "Since there is an impression that a practicable vaccine for poliomyelitis is either at hand or immediately around the corner, it may be best to start this discussion with the statement that such a vaccine is not now at hand and that one can only guess as to what is around the corner. . . . Unquestionably, the ultimate goal for the prevention of poliomyelitis is immunization with 'living' avirulent virus which will confer immunity for many years or for life." Six months later, Sabin endorsed a joint statement by leading American virologists saying that Salk's "formalin-inactivated vaccine is insufficiently tested for mass trial, potentially unsafe, of undetermined potency, and of undetermined stability," and that it should not be distributed to children.

Was Salk, in trying to rush his research to make a vaccine to give to hundreds of thousands of children, working too fast?

Some of us might say: Not fast enough.

sixteen

I first returned to school electronically: American Telephone and Telegraph had just developed a two-way speaker system that could be activated over a phone line. These days we call it a speakerphone. I had what must have been one of the first ones. On my desk in my bedroom was a device about the size of a bread box, with a speaker and a button I could press when I wanted to speak. At school was another such box that picked up the voices in my classroom and, when I pressed the button at my end, broadcast my voice to the room. My friend Jim carried the box from classroom to classroom for me, and so I began to attend my classes in the winter.

This device had only one drawback. When the teacher asked me a question and I started to answer, if I cheated by opening a book the damned device broadcast the sound of turning pages. I had to learn to let up on the button whenever I turned a page and then push the button when I resumed speaking so that my page turning was done in silence. In this way, even though I had missed the early part of the semester, I was able to answer questions as well as anyone who had not missed any school at all. My teachers pretended they didn't know I was doing this, and my classmates enjoyed my delinquency.

After a few months of school in this way, and with continuing practice at walking and the purchase of a backpack for my books, I was ready in the early spring to go back to school every day.

Here's what school was like. From the pages of the Barrington High School student newspaper, the *Broncho*, that my mother saved for me, I am reminded that this is the world I longed to re-enter, and these are the lives I envied:

Betty Johansen likes college weekends, convertibles, gray Buicks, senior parties, potlucks, and slumber parties. Betty's hobbies are telling jokes, giving parties, and doing plays.

Donna's ideal men are Jack Webb and Bugs Bunny, and her favorite songs are "It Had to Be You," "Side by Side," and "Bunny Hop."

Cis Buckley likes Ike, weekends, senior parties, and Phi Delta. Steak is her favorite food. Cis's unusual incident was breaking a bed out at Lorrie's. Among her favorite songs is "Why Don't You Believe Me?" Her aim is to go to college, preferably Northwestern. Her advice to underclassmen is: "Study now, because you can't learn it all in your senior year."

Bill Jepson is the only boy on the cheerleading team. He likes cheerleading, square dancing, world history, lunch, "I Love Lucy," and Monopoly. He dislikes grammar and onion soup. His aim in life is to be a peanut picker in Mongolia, and his ideal woman is Dagmar's grandmother.

Yvonne likes Ray, football, Ray, basketball, Ray, Lincolns, Ray, track, Ray, cheering, Ray, food, Ray, music, and Ray. "Tenderly" is her favorite song. To graduate, earn a mint, and have thirteen kids (twelve boys and one girl—a football team, one sub, and a cheerleader) is her aim in life.

Nancy Mac likes hotrods, house parties, weekends, Florida, drive-ins, and custom cars. She dislikes school, parasites, nosey people, and people who gossip! Her favorite foods are hamburgers, Cokes, french fries, pot roast, and fudge. Among her favorite songs is "Why Don't You Believe Me?"

Bill Carter's favorite music is Rachmaninoff's Concerto No. 2 in C Minor and the Cincinnati Syncopated Garbage Can Bounce.

George Heiland likes hunting, women, hotrods, women, money, and women. His biggest dislike is people who won't believe his car will turn 110 in 60 seconds from a standing start.

In this world, the highest virtue was perkiness, and its close relatives: cheerfulness, chipperness, and bounciness. The first hula hoop went on the market in the fifties ($1.98 each), and the first Barbie doll; NASA asked for applications from anyone who wanted to be an astronaut; the United States Patent Office granted a patent to Bertha Dlugi for bird diapers; and the most popular activity on college campuses was to see how many guys could fit into a single telephone booth (the record: significant portions of thirty-four guys at Modesto Junior College, with the booth lying sideways on the ground).

The normal diet was the same that would turn up several years later as the list of pantry items Elvis made sure were on hand "at all times, every day" at Graceland: hamburgers, Pepsi, hot dogs, peanut butter, Spearmint and Doublemint and Juicy Fruit gum, and brownies every night.

An open letter from the cheerleaders to the editor of

the *Broncho*: "What did you think of last weekend's games, or
didn't you see them? Well, if you didn't go to the games, you
can shake hands with half the student body, they didn't go
either. Some of the kids, or rather a lot of them, when asked
whether they went to the last game, said, 'Oh, I had a date,' or
'I didn't have any way to get there.' Sure you had a date, but
what's wrong with going to a basketball game on a date? As for
not having a ride, you can always ask around and find one,
that is if you really want one. . . .

"If the team thinks that the game is important enough to
play, then the student body should think it important enough
to attend and show their school spirit. We've got a terrific
team, one of the best around here, so why do we hesitate to
get out and support them? To have top teams, we've got to
have a winning student body that wants its teams to come out
ahead. In order to do this, we all must get out to the games,
and above all, cheer the teams on to *victory*."

Here is my classmate Bill Dow's poem "America":

Many people from many lands
Are living here as one.
They work together, learn together
For them living is fun.

This nation of ours is a powerful one,
It's known from shore to shore.
But as it grows, as everyone knows,
Cooperation is needed even more.

Rivers, valleys, mountains, plains,
Make up our beautiful land.

America is a wonderful place,
Made by God's own hand.

From the column of the Inquiring Reporter: "What do you think of our President-elect?"

Sandra Tate: "I think Ike will make a wonderful President and is the man our country needs."

Mary Beckhart: "I think he's great!"

Judy Gould: "I think it was great."

Bob Goldman: "I personally think Stevenson was more informed, but I wish Ike all the luck he needs."

Peter Devereaux: "I feel that President-elect Eisenhower will be compared with other great presidents such as Lincoln, Jefferson, and Washington. Now the men of college and high school age can be secure that the leader of our country will do everything possible to end the terrors of war. At least you can call America a unified democracy."

Jerry Jahnke: "I go Pogo!"

From the Karousing Kid: "Greetings Friends: Hey, you kids, what's the trouble? You sure turned out to be a dead bunch this week. Hardly any parties or anything. . . . There's one peppy group in the school and that's the team. Those were really swell games last week, weren't they? Just because they're so good is no sign to stop cheering them on. Be sure to come to the game this weekend."

Jim Tuohy wrote a letter to the editor of the *Broncho*:

"It is extremely doubtful that Senator Nixon did anything morally wrong in accepting over $18,000 used as an expense fund during less than two years he has been in the Senate.

"Although all elective officers accept contributions for campaigns, this is the first case of actual salary subsidy brought

to public light (there are probably very few, if any, others). . . .
Many of the Republicans' charges [against the Democrats] of
corruption [gifts to President and Mrs. Truman of a deep
freeze, a mink coat, and other items] are the same sort of thing
that this Nixon affair is—things that aren't really corruption
at all. . . .

"The expense fund incident is further evidence that men in
high, honorable, and responsible positions are woefully un-
derpaid. A Senator, for example, can hardly be expected to
maintain two homes on $12,000 a year. . . ."

Of the girls graduating from high school, Katherine Mc-
Cain hoped to be an English teacher and get married; Mary
Walbaum hoped to teach in elementary school and become "a
faithful PTA member as the mother of sixteen students";
Donna Schmidt wanted to swim and play tennis and work in
a hospital or nursery school with small children; Muffy Mot-
ter wanted to go to Florida and Nassau and then take courses
at Briarcliff Junior College; Karen Twerdahl hoped to study
liberal arts at Northwestern, have a job on a newspaper, and
then get married; Merrie Press hoped to be a model for a
couple of years before getting married; Joanne Peters hoped to
study liberal arts at Illinois Wesleyan, get married, and have
twins; Judy Kensel hoped to become a commercial artist and
"marry after college, maybe"; Betty Blaydes hoped to have a
career as a research chemist.

This is what they learned from the textbook they studied
in their home economics course:

1. Have dinner ready: Plan ahead, even the night before, to have a delicious meal—on time. This is a
   way of letting him know that you have been think-

ing about him, and are concerned about his needs. Most men are hungry when they come home and the prospects of a good meal are part of the warm welcome needed.

2. Prepare yourself: Take 15 minutes to rest so you will be refreshed when he arrives. Touch up your makeup, put a ribbon in your hair and be fresh looking. He has just been with a lot of work-weary people. Be a little gay [in the fifties this meant happy] and a little more interesting. His boring day may need a lift.

3. Clear away the clutter: Make one last trip through the main part of the house just before your husband arrives, gathering up school books, toys, paper, etc. Then run a dust cloth over the tables. Your husband will feel he has reached a haven of rest and order, and it will give you a lift, too.

4. Prepare the children: Take a few minutes to wash the children's hands and faces if they are small, comb their hair, and if necessary, change their clothes. They are little treasures and he would like to see them playing the part.

5. Minimize the noise: At the time of his arrival, eliminate all noise of washer, dryer, dishwasher or vacuum. Try to encourage the children to be quiet. Be happy to see him. Greet him with a warm smile and be glad to see him.

6. Some Don'ts: Don't greet him with problems or complaints. Don't complain if he's late for dinner. Count this as minor compared with what he might have gone through that day.

7. Make him comfortable: Have him lean back in a comfortable chair or suggest he lie down in the bedroom. Have a cool or warm drink ready for him. Arrange his pillow and offer to take off his shoes. Speak in a low, soft, soothing and pleasant voice. Allow him to relax and unwind.

8. Listen to him: You may have a dozen things to tell him, but the moment of his arrival is not the time. Let him talk first.

9. Make the evening his: Never complain if he does not take you out to dinner or to other places of entertainment; instead, try to understand his world of strain and pressure, his need to be home and relax.

10. The goal: Try to make your home a place of peace and order where your husband can relax.

The idea now was to find out what *I* could and couldn't do in every way for the rest of my life.

Here's what I couldn't do:

play football
play baseball
play basketball
run the high hurdles in track
run
jump
dance

Here's what I could do:

fifty pushups

fifty chinups

walk the length of a football field and not trip on the grass

carry plenty of books and papers in a backpack

tell jokes

read and write

go up and down stairs standing up, holding the banister

hold both crutches in one hand, take hold of the banister of a stairway in the other hand, and swing down three or four steps at a time, keeping up with the other kids on the stairways in high school

have a sword fight with my crutches—tossing one to another boy, holding on to a banister in a school stairwell, and having at each other with the thrust and parry of fencers

throw my crutches down a carpeted flight of stairs, and, holding on to the banister, lower myself abruptly to the stairs, and, seeming to fall headfirst (sliding on my stomach really), fling myself down the stairs in a horrifying clamor of thumping flesh and rattling crutches, turning round and round as I went down to the bottom, so that, although in time all my classmates knew I could do this and the shock value was gone, they would sometimes ask me to do it if their parents were home and were still among the naive

do square dance calls—especially singing square dance calls—for the high school exhibition square dance team, which often went out on trips to other high schools to put on shows, which meant traveling and

getting to spend time with the girls on the team
(Suzy Harvey was on the team)

act in high school plays such as *The Ghost of Gramercy
Park*, in which I played a ghost of a wounded Revo-
lutionary War soldier, and *The Little Foxes*, in which
I played the wheelchair-bound husband of the
dreadful Regina, and thus escape into other realities,
try new personae, and show off to girls (Suzy Harvey was in the casts)

accompany my pals to the local dump to find a toilet
bowl to place at the stately entrance of the suburban
headquarters of the American Can Company

get together with a few guys one evening and take food
coloring out of the kitchen cabinet and dye our hair
green and blue and red and yellow

with my buddies, steal three cannon from the local
cemetery and deliver them to the front porches of
the town mayor, chief of police, and, naturally, principal of the high school, leaving a note signed in the
blood of one of us that the South would rise again

Maybe the cannon episode was not such a bright idea—I
mean, compared to the others. Whether we quite consciously
registered the fact or not, we pulled the cannon prank the
night before Memorial Day, when many of the town's citizens, including the widows and children of men who had died
in World War II, marched to the cemetery for the annual
commemorative ceremony. The school authorities by now
knew who the incorrigible pranksters were and called us in; we
confessed, were put on trial in our local civil court, found
guilty, and sentenced to a year of probation, during which a

Cook County probation officer, accustomed to the tough cases of downtown Chicago, gave us a monthly lecture on the perils of statutory rape, an act that none of us had ever heard of, much less contemplated.

After that spring in high school, and regular therapy sessions to rebuild my muscles, by summer my right leg was strong enough to press both the accelerator and the brake in a car with automatic transmission. So I got my driver's license, and I took the car out and drove it as fast as it would go. I liked mobility. And speed. I did this until one evening, taking some friends to a drive-in movie, I passed a car on a hill and found myself going toward a head-on collision with a car in the oncoming lane. I could not get back into my own lane of traffic: the cars to my right were uncertain whether to slow down or speed up to let me back in, and so they left no space for me. Time shifted into slow motion, as it does in these moments, or the mind processes information with such terrific speed that, later on, when we recall the events, we recall more details than we ordinarily can recall of a few seconds' events. I pulled my car off onto the shoulder on the left-hand side—as did the oncoming car. I pulled the car back onto the road—as did the oncoming car. I feinted to the left shoulder again—as though it were a football game and I needed to fake out the tackler—and, as the oncoming car went to the left shoulder again, too, I pulled quickly back onto the road, and then into a hole that opened up for me in my lane of cars.

I was as calm and cold as I had been facing death in the isolation ward. Everyone else in the car was yelling and weeping and moving frantically around. But, on the theory that lightning never strikes twice in the same place, I thought I was invulnerable; I thought I'd had my bad thing happen to me.

And yet I knew that I, too, must be registering this frightening event somewhere in my psyche, so I calmly slowed the car
down, signaled the cars behind me, and pulled gently off the
road onto the right-hand shoulder. I put the car into Park and
turned off the engine, and then I shook uncontrollably for five
or ten minutes.

A few years ago I got to know a neurosurgeon who is up
every morning at five or six for surgery and who sees too many
patients who never recover. For him, he says, the happiest moment is when he sees a patient he has operated on begin to act
"badly," impatiently, like a delinquent, someone who doesn't
want to take her medicine anymore, or do what the doctor
tells her, who refuses to be a patient, and maybe even just gets
out of bed and walks out of the hospital in defiance of all the
doctor's orders. This, says my neurosurgeon friend, is the beginning of the flight toward health.

Sometimes I was indeed engaged in a flight toward health,
just feeling the pleasure of being out of the hospital, enjoying
the freedom, testing to see what I could do with my body
now. But, to tell the truth, at other times the behavior was
more like daring my body to fail me. And at still other times
it was revenge against the body that had failed me. I started
drinking Scotch, not for the pleasure of it, but to get drunk.

And at the same time, because I couldn't run from the dangers I created or consented to, I developed an ability to talk
fast, charm, lie, and smile. One night, Kinney Smith was driving his jeep out County Line Road with several of us riding
with him. The top was off the jeep, and I told him we could
see the beauty of the night better if he would turn off his headlights. He did, and suddenly we came up behind a car that was

stalled in the middle of the highway with its lights out. Kinney swerved, the jeep went up on two wheels, came back down, sideswiped the stalled car, and rocked from one side to the other before getting its equilibrium back. Kinney was all for running for it, but we persuaded him to stop to see if anyone had been hurt. Our friend Steve, who had had his foot out over the edge of the jeep, was lucky not to have lost his leg. Finally, Kinney stopped. And the other car, now running again, pulled up behind us. All the other guys got out of the jeep and ran into the woods, leaving me there to explain. I told a lot of lies, I don't remember what, and the other driver was ashen-faced and deeply apologetic for *his* mistake!

By the time a huge Confederate flag was taken way up to the top of the high school chimney and attached there to fly in the breeze, the Superintendent of Schools, Frank Thomas, didn't even need to inquire who had done it. Mr. Thomas was a big man, maybe six and a half feet tall, maybe 250 pounds, afraid of nothing really, certainly not intimidated by teenage boys. He had the flag brought to his office, hung it behind his desk, and invited Jim and Steve and a couple of others of our group into his office. He asked how everyone was doing, and said he hoped the boys understood that all he really cared about was that his students do well and not do anything where they could get seriously hurt. He didn't mention the flag.

For most of my high school years, I thought that my recovery from polio meant I was supposed to recover my former self, and the future my former self had once looked forward to. The assumption was: Life would return to normal if no one mentioned anything not normal. The fact that it was not mentioned, I think, made it an immensely powerful presence.

It was not possible to say: Well, my life is no longer normal, or no longer quite normal, or the idea of normal must be extended somehow to include the life I am now going to live, or who cares what is normal, I'm going to make a unique life, I'm going to embrace my difference and explore it and throw myself into a life like you've never seen before. No. It was simply assumed I would have a normal life.

The idea of the normal, and of its desirability, had been so deeply ingrained in me that I couldn't simply drop it—any more than high school girls could drop the standards of normality and desirability for a woman that they had learned in their home economics class. And yet the realness of my deviance from normality was so palpable, so present in my body every day, that I couldn't deny it. I've known other people— smarter, quicker, more robust than I am—who were able to just choose one or the other of these alternatives, the normal or the abnormal, and get on with their lives. Either one is a good choice, but I couldn't take either: both held me in such a grip. I remained suspended between the two, trying to work out some third way.

On Mondays, Wednesdays, and Fridays, I was normal. On Tuesdays, Thursdays, and Saturdays, I was a deviant, pulling pranks, driving fast, harboring the wish that I could bring the whole world down into wreckage. On some days I mixed the two: a veneer of normality with little outbursts and eruptions of delinquency. On Sundays, I rested, because this performance was exhausting.

I flailed. Sometimes I performed an intact outer self because it was what I wanted—to be normal and robust and optimistic. And sometimes I performed this self because it seemed the thing for a healthy person to do, and it was what others wanted of me. Some days I tried to find my own true path in life. I ran toward normality, and at the same time away from it, trying to pass for normal, and feeling it to be a lie.

In short, I had become a politician, living two lives at the same time. And so it seemed natural that I should run for office. And I did. I ran for president of the student council, and won. So then I ran for the presidency of the Northern Illinois district student council, and won. I was good at performing a public persona. So then I ran for the presidency of the Illinois state student council, and lost. The chat going around the caucus rooms was that I was foxy, trying to pretend I was someone I wasn't. They didn't know who I was or who I was trying to pretend to be, but they didn't like it.

Then, too, my project of compensation—using my mind and words and arguments in place of the strength of my body—was not always a happy choice. I found that sometimes I could unleash a cutting sentence in an argument. Or better yet, if I needed, I could conduct a Socratic dialogue in history class, speaking not just in sentences but in whole paragraphs, and bully others with a form of logic they had never heard before. I had never been a bully, and I knew it was wrong to use knowledge in this way. It dishonored the knowledge, and it tainted my relationship with it—and, for sure, it was not a good way to be liked, either. But still, sometimes I couldn't help myself. And if I'd had a day of feeling especially unequal to my classmates for one reason or another, if someone really crossed me, I could cut his heart out.

Through all this, Jim was my most loyal friend, the most loyal friend I've had in life, bringing me the Kinsey Report in the hospital, carrying the speakerphone from classroom to classroom, bringing my school assignments back and forth to

school for me. He couldn't keep me honest; that was too big
a job for anyone. But he did sustain me as I floundered. He
came over to my house to visit almost every evening after he
had had dinner. It became my mother's standing joke: Oh,
here's Jim, it must be dinnertime. And Jim would be offered
a chair and would sit down and eat a second dinner. He was,
at that time, a six-foot-tall sophomore basketball star, on his
way to six feet four in what seemed only a matter of weeks. In
fact, he was growing so quickly that, sometimes, he would be
taking the basketball down the court, with no other player
within yards of him, and suddenly he would fall to the floor
in a tangle of arms and legs, having tripped over his own fast-
growing feet.

It was because of his friendship and loyalty that my own
first forays out into the world that winter and spring had been
to basketball games. The car could be pulled right up to the
door of the gym, where the polished floors were even smoother
than those at the hospital. In time, after the games I would go
to a party at someone's house.

By the time I could drive a car myself, I was independent
again. Suzy Harvey and I began dating. She was a cheerleader,
which is to say, she was not only pretty and energetic and
popular, she was also the mainstream.

These were the official qualifications for a good cheerleader, according to the *Broncho*:

1. A pleasing personality
2. A good personal appearance
3. Imagination and resourcefulness
4. Organizing ability and leadership
5. Ability and control of the body

6. A commanding voice with volume
7. The desire to cheer for the team, not for personal glory
8. At least average ability, scholastically
9. Willingness to devote time to further the squad
10. Character which reflects well upon the school

Suzy took me into the mainstream with her. She had a sexiness and vitality, a brightness and enthusiasm that was life itself. I don't know what I brought to her, but she brought a lot to me.

Gail Bias, the girl who had reconstructive surgeries, said that when she was a teenager, she didn't want to go to a school dance, because of her limp, because everyone stared at her. It was easier for a boy. Suzy and I went to the junior prom. I wore a white summer tuxedo jacket. Suzy wore a white off-the-shoulder dress with a thousand crinoline slips underneath it, white satin shoes with little straps at heel and toe. She had very short hair then, and a long, smooth neck, like a young swan. We danced. That is, she moved with me. I had figured out how, with one hand on her waist and my other hand steadying myself by holding my own hip, I could stand and move a few steps without my crutches. She let one arm rest lightly on my shoulder, one hand took me lightly but supportively at the waist, and we moved together to the music.

seventeen

For the rest of his life after I had polio, my father carried a picture of me in his wallet that he had taken at the halftime of a football game. I was sitting on the grass with my teammates while the coach talked to us. My father had come around to the side of the group, and as I turned to look at him, he took the picture: an adolescent boy in the vigor of youth, a strong jaw and neck, a crew cut, massive shoulders with the football pads, and not a football-playing meathead but a moderately intelligent-looking boy.

He carried this picture of me, and no other, because, I think, that was the last moment when my father felt uncomplicated pride in me. Ever after, his feelings were mixed with regret, and, as I felt more and more that I needed to find my own way and that way was foreign to him, his feelings were mixed, too, with incomprehension and sadness at the distance and rejection. I always took the fact that he carried that picture with him as a sign of his disappointment in me, and it filled me with rage. In the last years of his life, we became very close, relaxed with each other, reassured simply by being near each other. But the photograph was still on a table not far from his bed when he died at the age of ninety-four.

For this reason, and I'm sure for others, I learned to pose

for photographs in such a way that my crutches didn't show. Usually I would toss one crutch off to the side, and stand with the remaining crutch just behind one leg so that it was invisible. When I was photographed sitting, I made sure the crutches were not in the frame. I knew that there was a reason to be embarrassed that I was crippled.

But I'm not the only one who did this. Even Franklin Roosevelt, as public as he was in starting the polio rehabilitation clinic at Warm Springs, as important a figure as he was in opening the way into the mainstream for the disabled people who came after him, would never allow photographers to take his picture when he was *struggling*. Whenever he emerged from an automobile, he had several aides surround the car door as he threw his clumsy legs out of the car, grimaced at the difficulty of getting temporarily to his feet, and, with the occasional look of anxiety on his face, twisted clumsily to be lowered into his wheelchair. This was photographed only once or twice when his distracted aides were unable to block it. What was photographed repeatedly was the smiling, vigorous president in his convertible, with his cigarette holder held jauntily in his teeth, and then, moments later, the triumphant, energetic president sitting upright in his chair (with its small wheels tucked in almost invisibly under the chair).

In a photograph that was taken of Roosevelt visiting children at Warm Springs, a little girl with withered legs and a little boy with a blanket over his legs sit in wheelchairs smiling at the president, who sits in a regular armchair, dressed in a sleek business suit, his wheelchair nowhere to be seen.

And he had his metal leg braces painted black at the ankles so they would not shine but rather they would disappear against his black socks.

My father was angry at my crutches. The crutches were adjustable: a smaller aluminum tube slid up and down inside a larger one to modify the length; the tubes were held in place with a movable steel pin inserted through one of a half-dozen holes drilled in the tubes. These pins would sometimes break, or work against the holes until they were loose, and then my father would take me and my crutches down to the local blacksmith, who would put a steel bolt through the crutch. In time, I had a half-dozen ugly bolts inflicted on each of the original ugly crutches. My father never bought me a new pair of crutches. His anger against the crutches was as great as mine, and he punished the crutches with these steel bolts.

In time, on my own, and over the objection of my doctors, who feared I would throw my back out, I learned to walk with one Canadian crutch in my right hand (more recently, my snappy fire-engine-red designer crutch), and a wooden cane in my left, and this was the handiest of all. I could—and can—hook the cane in my back pocket when I need to, so that I have one hand free to shake hands or hold a drink at a cocktail party.

My parents, having held out against quackery and heroic experimental treatments for well over a year after I got out of the hospital, finally could not resist trying something. They drove me up to Milwaukee, where the world-famous surgeon Wally Blount had his orthopedic practice. It turned out that Dr. Blount was the originator and finest practitioner of the tensor fascia lata muscle transplant. (Sookie had made a beautiful anatomical drawing of the muscles of the human body for me and put it up on my bedroom wall, so that I knew—to the surprise of Dr. Blount—just what muscles he was talking about, and how to say their Latin names.) This was the surgery in which the tensor fascia lata, the outermost sheath of muscle in the thigh, is cut away from its attachment to the knee, split in half, and one of its ends is attached to the rib cage, the other taken across the abdomen and attached to the opposite hip arch.

To show me just how effective this surgery would be in strengthening and stabilizing my torso, and thus make it easier for me to walk, Dr. Blount said an assistant would put tape from my thigh to my rib cage and across my abdomen so that I could see how much better I could walk. I stripped, and the assistant taped me up, while Dr. Blount spoke more medical terms to my parents who, smart as they were, didn't understand him. "There," he said, when the taping was finished. "Now walk up and down the hallway and show your mother and father how much better you walk."

I went up and down the hallway, and, although I wanted this to work and, even more than that, wanted to be polite to the great surgeon — after all, what did I know? — and, even more than that, wanted to give good news to my parents, who had gone to so much trouble and were about to go to so much expense for me, I had to admit I didn't notice any difference.

"Come over here," said Dr. Blount angrily. And he himself taped me up, a good bit more roughly than his assistant had, with many layers of tape.

"Now walk," he said.

Under the influence of his anger and the loving hope of my parents, I said I thought this might have made some slight difference.

"Well, you'll see," said Dr. Blount. "After the surgery, you'll notice a tremendous improvement."

I've known people since, I should say, who were social

friends of Dr. Blount, and did consider him a great doctor and a fine person. He was, in some sense, sacrificing himself to his career of healing. He had Parkinson's disease, which made his right hand—his cutting hand—shake uncontrollably. All the while he talked to me, he held his right hand in his left, to hold down the shaking a little bit. Before surgery, I was told, he took an injection of heroin, which gave him a steady hand. So he was, by this time, a habitual heroin user.

Whenever I walk into a hospital, I'm overcome at once with a sense of peace, security, well-being. Back in this familiar place where I didn't die, I feel safe. I know this is wrong of me, but I can't get over it. I know the routines and the language of hospitals, I feel real affection for nurses, and, like most of the kids I knew in the hospital, I came to feel that the doctors, even those who performed unnecessary surgery, were doing the best they could given their limitations of knowledge and character.

Dr. Blount was followed on his rounds at the hospital by eight or ten surgeons from all over the world, surgeons from Germany and France and England and India and China, who had come to see how he worked, and how he performed his famous muscle transplants. I was glad to have such a celebrity for a doctor, though I confess, whenever he put his shaking hand on my arm to reassure me, I thought he might be Groucho Marx visiting children in hospitals.

After the surgery, I spent a couple of months recuperating in the hospital—all those muscles healing themselves into new places. Of course, the operation didn't work a bit. I told my mother and father that it was a big improvement, I lied to my father about it till the day he died, but the surgery was completely useless.

Dr. Blount, however, proud of his work, kept inviting me back to Milwaukee whenever he brought together a group of doctors from around the world, to put me on stage in the medical theater. I would arrive early, strip, and put on a little loincloth, like a diaper. This in itself was a disagreeable experience. I was, in any case, an embarrassable adolescent boy. But to be reduced to an object, as these days, finally, everyone knows, is profoundly diminishing. In fact, I was reduced to something even less than an object: I was a specimen.

I was brought out on stage, like the elephant man, and Dr. Blount would indicate my assorted parts with a wooden pointer as he described his surgery to the physicians. Sometimes the physicians would be invited up on stage to poke me and probe me. I would be asked only one question by the audience: Was I able to walk better now? And I would invariably answer yes. But after I had done this a number of times, it occurred to me that if I told the truth I would not be asked back again. It occurred to me, too, that my parents were not in the room for this show, so they wouldn't hear me say it had been worthless. Nor, I realized, would Dr. Blount ever tell them I had said it. So one time, asked the inevitable question, this time by a surgeon from France, I said, as casually as I could, "No, I don't think it has made any difference at all, really; maybe I'm a *little* worse." I was never asked to return.

Dr. Blount wanted me to come back for surgery to fuse the bones in my left hip. The idea was that by immobilizing the hip, I wouldn't have any flexibility in it; the thigh would be fixed permanently, coming straight down from the pelvic bone, so that when I sat down, I would have to slump down, sitting more on the small of my back than on my buttocks; the good part, according to Dr. Blount, was that my left leg would be stabilized. In time, possibly the left knee could be made immobile, so that the whole leg from hip to shin would be rendered a sturdy post. My mother and father asked me if I thought I wanted to do this, and I said I wasn't so sure; they never raised the subject again.

"At some point," as Daniel J. Wilson has written about boys and girls recovering from polio, "in every case, constraints appeared. The extent of the destruction became apparent; progress in recovery slowed and came to a halt."

And at some point, as Fred Davis has written, "the paralysis must be accepted as a given and efforts made to work around it or to compensate for it; it cannot be done away with."

eighteen

I fled into my own mind, and I discovered there the deep pleasures of solitude, the pleasures hermits must know, a world cut free of all physical limitation, a world where, in the imagination, anything is possible, a world where all bodies are equal, where the mind can take flight, and where it can find a quiet place for solitary reflection.

And I discovered the pleasures of books, of reading quietly by myself, able to travel effortlessly, swiftly, anywhere in the world, to the deepest inner passions, to the furthest reaches of abstract ratiocination. I came to love not only the experience of reading, but the touch of books, the lusciousness of a beautiful binding, the grace or boldness or heft of typefaces, the swirl of a decorative device at the heading of a chapter, the discretion of the page number placed diplomatically in the corner, present if one wants it, making itself tactfully invisible otherwise — perfect butlers, these page numbers are — the smell of a new book, the alarmed crack of its binding if you open it too violently, the curve of its pages if you lay the book gently open on a table. This is why people say the Internet cannot replace books, because we are of a time when people came to love books the way they love human flesh and grass and trees. Each one of us, at one time or another, discovered in books our most secret selves, that part of ourselves the world despised or couldn't understand, some tender or vulnerable part that found companionship only in a book, and so we fell in love with books and can't bear to part with them. There is love of another person, and there is love of books. These are the two great loves of life. Anyone who has ever felt like an outsider knows this.

Imagine. There was once a time, before the late Middle Ages, when hardly anyone read. Or, when they did read, they read out loud to one another, so that the experience of reading was a social event, and no doubt an event that had its distinct pleasures, but not an event where one could sink into one's own thoughts for as long as one might want, let the mind go off on a path of its own without being called back to the shared ideas of the society. The social historian Philippe Ariès has written that the " 'privatization' of reading is undeniably one of the major cultural developments of the early modern era."

Silent reading, Ariès says, "radically transformed intellectual work, which in essence became an intimate activity, a personal confrontation with an ever-growing number of texts. . . . It made possible a more personal form of piety" and a more personal form of thought. Private reading "paved the way for previously unthinkable audacities."

Montaigne thought of books as a refuge. "When at home," he said, "I turn aside . . . to my library . . . which I like for being a little hard to reach and out of the way."

Montaigne's library, Ariès said—but really every library— is a place from which one can see without being seen, which confers a kind of power in addition to its other pleasures. The eye can take in shelves of human secrets at a single glance—

all of them available, all open to the one who knows where to find them. Here is a chance to know all the human heart without the constraint of supervision, telling us what we may or may not know or feel or think. There is no correct feeling in a library: rage, remorse, pity, hope, love, all these things can be deeply felt, with no one saying to us, "Get over it."

I had no library, no study, but I had bookshelves in my bedroom, and that became my refuge. I spent time with Montaigne and Shakespeare and the Greeks; we spoke as equals—if not in talents, then in interests and passions. There is a wonderful, voluptuous painting by Jean-François de Troy called *Reading Molière*. A man sits at the center of a group of five women. Another stands just outside the circle. They are all dressed in gorgeous early-eighteenth-century silks and velvets. The men have those telltale ruffled lace cuffs that come down onto their hands almost to their fingertips, signifying that they were unable to do any labor at all—even the labor of holding an ink pen—except for the labor of thinking and conversing. The women, whose dresses of Chinese silk, with embroidery work of flowers or of stars deep in space, are themselves whole worlds of mysterious allure. The man at the center of the painting holds a book from which he is reading, and the women are all lying back languidly in their chairs as though they had all just made love all afternoon. This is a social reading, not the modern private affair, but it conjured up nicely the sort of group—in slightly different dress, and from different epochs, and, often, with a different ratio of the genders—that I sometimes conjured up in my imagination in my bedroom on an afternoon, all of us together, from different times and places, enjoying one another's company.

Reading books of magic, like Prospero did, was once the

paradigm for all reading, according to Ariès; it was an activity that almost had to be done in private, and that "conferred upon the reader a dangerous power." Certainly I noticed that my father, a devout Catholic, had come to worry that I might happen upon a book that was listed on the church's Index of Forbidden Books.

My Virgil in this descent into the world of books was Alan Peshkin, a history teacher who was the faculty adviser to the student council. As the council's adviser, Mr. Peshkin was obliged to become my adviser when I was elected president of the Northern Illinois District student council. The district council's monthly executive committee meetings took place in Chicago. So one Saturday each month, Mr. Peshkin and I would drive down to Chicago. And the very first time we did this, Mr. Peshkin asked me, after the meeting, if I would like to go with him to a secondhand bookstore. There were many secondhand bookstores in Chicago, Mr. Peshkin said, and he knew where the best ones were. He made his invitation in the tone of voice and with the manner a teacher might use if he were offering cocaine to a student, or sex. I understood, when I said yes, that we were about to enter some other realm together.

When we arrived at the bookstore, he gave me ten dollars— to get me started, he said; if we came back, I should bring my own money. I asked him what books I could buy. He didn't understand the question. I meant could I buy history or philosophy or biography. He said, "You can buy anything you like." I felt almost faint.

He told me I should not waste big money on the standard works I would need for my basic library. You could find old copies of Plato and Aristotle for a dime or a quarter. I should save the big chunks of money for the more unusual purchases, for some rare or new volume that might cost as much as two dollars.

A. J. Liebling, a young man when his father sent him to the Sorbonne, tells in the book he wrote about the experience, *Between Meals: An Appetite for Paris*, that his father gave him a monthly allowance adequate to survive on, but not so generous that he could live extravagantly. And, Liebling said, he thought that it gave him the perfect means to further his education as a gourmet. He never went to classes; he spent his time eating in restaurants. And because his funds were sufficient but limited, he was faced constantly with such choices as whether to splurge on the truffles and drink a cheap wine or sacrifice the truffles for something less expensive and have a really good Bordeaux or Burgundy. He felt it forced him to be a connoisseur in the way that either too little or too much money would not have.

The same principle operated in my book runs with Alan Peshkin. I put together a remarkable library over the months. We brought back one or two boxes each month; each month's haul contained the current bargains in dime and quarter immortals, along with some lesser works, minor histories of the Renaissance, biographies of less than essential figures. I traveled in my reading from the philosophy of Plato and Aristotle through most of Western philosophy, and then to history, and at last to biography—from the realm of pure thought back to the world of daily life.

Along the way, I stumbled upon things that seemed to have been written for me. By purest chance, I found Georg

Büchner's *Woyzeck*—the play that Büchner left unfinished in his desk drawer when he died at the age of twenty-three, a play whose scenes break off suddenly in midsentence, where bits of scenes occur out of place, inexplicable things happen; a play composed of chunks and shards, broken pieces, raw, awkward, clumsy, with events crashing into one another without reason or cause; a shattered world, fucked up and roughhewn. As I would see some years later, many directors take this play and try to fix it. They remove the chunks of broken, pointless scenes; they make a more logical order of what remains, they put in transitions from one moment to the next, they smooth it out, they make it "work." In short, they kill it. From the first time I read it, I loved it: it felt to me exactly like life itself, with all its anguish and ruin and love—not like the well-made plays I saw in high school productions, or later in professional ones, even plays that present themselves as modern or avant-garde but really reduce themselves to the same standards of good play-making, the same pre-existing rules of normality and goodness by which I am judged and found wanting. Well-made plays feel hostile to me, as though they would suffocate me. Büchner left me free to make a whole life from ruins.

I was drawn strongly, too, to histories of the Renaissance. I wasn't conscious at first of the reasons I found the Renaissance so fascinating, but I came to think of it as my special epoch. It had followed hard on the heels of the Black Death that swept Europe in the fourteenth century, and it could be seen as the world's recovery from a dread disease into a new life. It had drawn people's attention from heaven to earth, from the powers of the divine to the immense powers of the natural, from the realm of the ideal to the realm of the real, from old things of value to new things of value. My effort to understand and embrace the Renaissance was in some way an effort to embrace life itself, my own rebirth.

My father was mildly positive about all this book buying, even though he sensed that it was taking me away from him, until the day he noticed I had brought home a copy of Machiavelli's *The Prince*, and then he exploded. Did I know this book was on the Index? What was I thinking? He would call Alan Peshkin and ask him what the hell *he* was thinking. Certainly this was the end of my book buying. Why did I want to have anything to do with this filthy book anyhow?

Somewhere, instinctively, I think I felt if I simply gave in to my father about this, I would be giving away my only chance for a feeling of strength and freedom in my life.

I said I didn't think it was filthy.

He said it was on the Index.

I asked him whether he knew what it was about, whether he had read it.

He said certainly not, it was on the Index.

I said then he didn't know what was objectionable about it, maybe nothing was, maybe something had been hundreds of years ago but was no longer, and someone had just forgotten to take it off the Index.

He didn't think so.

I left the room in anger and hopelessness.

He subsided. I heard him talking to my mother, gradually calming down.

I kept the book.

We hardly ever spoke of books again, not for twenty years.

I remember hearing a conversation once, about why so many Irish people become writers. One of the people in that conversation said: Oh, well, you know the only book most

Irish could afford to own was the Bible, and then the English forbade them to have Bibles in their homes, so they always knew the word was valuable and immensely powerful.

And although I couldn't play football and basketball, I discovered that I could write about them with real sympathy and passion, and so, without ever meaning to, I became a writer.

I became a writer before I had any plan about it. It felt good, and so I kept doing it. I wrote about sports for Barrington's weekly newspaper, and I found I liked putting together a sentence that moved and worked as well as a jump shot.

Here was something I could do with my head. And the page was, as they say, a level playing field. There I could be as good as anyone else, and maybe even better. After I had written about sports for a while, I tried short stories and poems.

Now and then I would tell my friends that I might become a writer. And sometimes someone would reply: "What do you have to say?"

I had nothing to say; it was just something I could do sitting down. It wasn't until years later I realized that writing is not about saying something, it is about discovering something.

nineteen

Like water seeking its own level, I was sinking, I mean sinking, gradually, without my quite realizing it, into the world that had become, as though by nature, mine, the world of the people who read books, the nonphysical people, the strange people, the deviants, the eggheads, the queers. Before I had polio, I hadn't known they were there. Now they reached out to me and took me in, made me feel comfortable, one of their own; they gave me a place where I belonged and was liked. These were the people who welcomed me. They were my good friends.

One of those at the center of this subterranean world was Ricky, an older boy who lived in the countryside just outside Barrington and had his own little room out in the horse barn where he smoked a pipe and collected all sorts of books of forbidden knowledge. It was a world as exotic as an opium den, furnished with old broken-down easy chairs and velvet drapes. He didn't collect pornography, although he had a few magazines of the kind with pictures of lightly clad girls that has disappeared nearly entirely these days except in catalogues meant mostly for women's eyes, the catalogues for Victoria's Secret and Frederick's of Hollywood ("Even in Hollywood," a picture caption in one of Ricky's *Caper* magazines said, "there are few girls who can match the loveliness of Marguerite Empey, our December cover girl. But this gal is endowed with more than her fair share of beauty. She also possesses a quality that delights discerning photographers and her public as well. This quality is a unique mobility of face and body that permits her to assume almost any maidenly characteristic at will. As the pictures on these and the preceding pages disclose, the lovely Miss Empey can be demure and wholesome, or sophisticated and sexy, or gay or moody; a word from the photographer and she is any or all of these.")

But Ricky's main collection was composed of books on magic tricks, the occult, Zen Buddhism; and books by people I'd never heard of before: Burton's *Anatomy of Melancholy*, Voltaire's dictionary, things by eighteenth-century philosophers who called themselves Deists. A group of us found each other at Ricky's: George Merritt, Dave Grinstead, Steve Hoffman, Mike Burleigh, and my lifelong friend Jim, whose basketball-playing place in the mainstream was always tentative because of the delinquent behavior he could not keep himself from falling into time and again.

George brought to these late-night drinking and smoking sessions an idea for traffic control, for the design of freeways and of inner-city traffic, which was a live issue at that time, since President Eisenhower was in the process of building what became the interstate highway system. George's design was based on Dante's *Divine Comedy,* some complicated notion he had about how the circles of hell in *The Divine Comedy* actually described a perfect traffic control system. George tried obsessively to explain this idea to the rest of us, and we tolerated him, the way orderlies in a mental institution humor the patients. When the Inquiring Reporter from the *Broncho* asked some of the kids what they thought of the plans for an addition to the high school, everyone thought it was a swell idea and terrific and worth the expense and hoped it could be finished soon. George said, "What do the coaches need new offices for? What is the school gymnastic room for? What about the room below the lobby? How about more classrooms?"

We were all autodidacts, knowing more than we were able to pronounce. If George spoke of Goethe, there was no one in his world who knew enough to tell him it was Ger-teh, not Go-ee-thee. It made all of us a little self-conscious, a little afraid to speak, to say what we knew, because we were aware that maybe some people did know how to pronounce these words, people we might run into by mistake, somebody's mother or father, true sophisticates, who got their knowledge of the world from the world instead of books and who lived among people who knew how to say things. My head swam in unpronounceable words, and still does.

Dave Grinstead, who spent a lot of time wandering around town with a sketchbook in his pocket, drawing people and places, otherwise liked to stay home and read the Encyclopedia Britannica. He said he was up to the letter E and he planned to go all the way. He had a remarkable memory for all he had read, and so he was completely unfit for normal high school society.

Steve Hoffman read history. I mean he read nothing else. And he read constantly. He was smart and odd, having come to all his ideas himself and never having had anyone to test them against. His knowledge of history was at a college level, or even a postgraduate level, so his peers couldn't begin to speak with him, and the teachers didn't have the time to correct his harebrained interpretations of things. His academic career in high school was rocky, and he was later expelled from the first college he attended because, having already acquired one warning after another from the dean's office for staying in his room to read instead of attending classes, he inadvertently started to read *War and Peace* one morning in the bathroom and, not realizing how much time was passing until he was far into the book, missed a final exam.

Mike Burleigh, the son of a lawyer, had the manner of Oscar Wilde. His idiosyncrasies were not as easy to pin down as those of George or Dave or Steve; he was an all-purpose deviant, sly, cynical, sneering, worldly, extravagant, limp-wristed — European in some way, sophisticated, with all the characteristics of a queen, although no one bothered to wonder if he was queer.

Bob Seaver, at that time several years out of college, would sometimes hang out with this group or play the elder sage to it. He was so far into the closet that even he didn't know he was homosexual in those days, though he did know that not all his interests were completely conventional, and he enjoyed being not quite in the mainstream. He had gone to Harvard and brought his college library back home with him; he was the kind of person, rare among the grown-ups I knew in Barrington, who read poetry for pleasure, memorized it, quoted it, loved it, and lived a life that suggested there was an alternative to the sort of grown-up life I mostly saw in Barrington.

"In recent years," as Fred Davis has written, "a more sophisticated approach to the study of deviance has become evident in social science. The works of Lemert, Becker, Cohen, Cloward, and Goffman have been in the forefront of a growing number of attempts to view this phenomenon from a broader, less parochial perspective, one in which deviance and deviant processes are treated as integral parts of the functioning of institutions and social structures. Prior to this, and even today, the predominant orientation in American social science has been to regard deviance almost exclusively in terms of the pathological, the abnormal, the psychologically unstable—at best, as an unwholesome, though perhaps unwilling, departure from social norms. In line with this conception, the tendency of countless researches in this field, on subjects ranging from breakfast-food choices to bureaucratic decision-making, has been to search for the roots of deviance in such entities as basic personality, childhood experience, and unconscious motivation.

". . . it is to the credit of the writers mentioned above that they have shifted the topic away from a predominantly pathological locus to a level at which it is conceived as a constituent element in social process—a ubiquitous, and perhaps necessary, accompaniment to group life." He could have asked me.

In truth, though I didn't know about it at the time, there were some real hardcore deviants in America in the fifties whose lives and work, like those of my friends in Barrington, were going to make the world more accommodating for me and for others who suffered from some form of difference. It was in the mid-fifties that Jack Kerouac published *On the Road*; that James Dean starred in *Rebel Without a Cause*; that Marlon Brando became an icon of alienation; that Betty Friedan began to write *The Feminine Mystique*, challenging the very heart of the world of Ozzie and Harriet; that Allen Ginsberg published *Howl*. The badge of a certifiable hardcore deviant was an FBI file, and Ginsberg had one in fairly short order, which said he was "subversive" and "potentially dangerous," a possible threat to the president of the United States, a person with "evidence of emotional instability (including unstable residence and employment record)," who had on occasion "chanted unintelligible poems," who had made "expressions of strong or violent anti-U.S. sentiment," and had an "antipathy toward good order and government." It was on December 5, 1955, that Martin Luther King, defending the right of Rosa Parks to sit in the white section of a bus in Montgomery, Alabama, became the voice of a more inclusive country; and it was in the mid-fifties that Robert Rauschenberg began to make art by picking stuff up off the street, broken stuff, rejected stuff—junk—and putting it into paintings and sculptures, saying: This, too, belongs in a museum; this, too, is worthy of attention and respect; this is the stuff of which great art can be made, great thoughts and feelings, astonishing pleasures, art that feels fresh, vigorous, unafraid, liberated, inclusive, democratic, free, beautiful.

The fifties was not an undifferentiated era of conformity; a great change was already under way, one of the most fundamental transformations in America in my lifetime—not an advance in technology, nor a growth in productivity, nor a new strategic place for America in the world, but more fundamental than any of those: a change of mind.

According to W. T. Lhamon, a professor of English at Florida State University, even the pop culture of the fifties was itself subversive, in a wonderfully underhanded way, of the very mainstream culture from which it sprang. As television took over America in the fifties (in 1950, 10 percent of the nation's homes had TVs; by the end of the decade, 86 percent did), the gatekeepers of the elite culture were simply bypassed. No one cared if television critics thought *Ozzie and Harriet* and *Father Knows Best* and *This Is Your Life* and *The Mickey Mouse Club* and *Captain Kangaroo* and *Wyatt Earp* and *Gun-*

smoke were stupid; we watched them anyway and loved them. No one cared if design critics thought the cars of the era were vulgar excrescences; we loved them. No one cared if Elvis Presley struck cultural commentators as repellent. And as the old standards of judgment were increasingly thought to be irrelevant to people who wanted to make up their own minds about what resonated with them, pop culture eroded all authority and so, even as it was mindless and stupid, it was also liberating, and helped to pave the way for an open society capable of embracing a multiplicity of values.

My political friends tell me that, in truth, we have not become liberated so much as Madison Avenue has absorbed deviance and difference and dissent into its marketing strategy and repackaged them as a salable lifestyle—hyping the *feeling* of liberation to reimprison the same old consumerist wage slaves. I can buy this, in part. But, in my bones, I feel different in the world now. I am more comfortable here. What Elvis and his contemporaries did was not mere style. I didn't know this at the time. At the time, I hated Elvis.

And I was certainly not the man Rauschenberg was. In the mid-fifties, I had not heard of him yet. Still caught in conflicted wishes to be free to be myself and, at the same time, to make my way in my father's world, I perceived that there was still a line somewhere on the margins I didn't want to cross, even though I didn't know why. My classmate Debbie Doolen had an older brother, Mark, who was a figure of some nervous curiosity among my friends. We often went over to Debbie's house for parties, but we never saw her brother. He was always upstairs and never came down. Or, once in a great while, he would come halfway down the stairs and peer at the young teenagers without speaking and then, after a half hour or so, go back up to his room. Everyone was afraid of him, like they would be of someone who lived in the attic and might be a deranged killer. Debbie's father decided at some point that I might become his son's friend, and I was invited over one afternoon for that purpose. Mark came halfway down the stairs, holding a book in one hand. We were introduced, and he said something about the subject of the history book he was reading, something about the French Revolution, I think. I had no idea what he was talking about, but I did think that whatever he was saying was even more sophisticated than the kind of things Steve was always saying. I couldn't respond. We had an awkward conversation. I thought he seemed entirely normal—very shy, some sort of geek, but perfectly normal. But we had nothing in common, and we both drew back from friendship. That was our only attempt at it.

I had a fear around this friendship with Mark that was being urged on me, a fear of being thought part of a narrowly defined group—and what was even worse, a group for which normal people felt some measure of pity. Or what was even worse than that, a group of people who felt pity for themselves. In *The Iceman Cometh*, Eugene O'Neill called it "bum pity"—the pity derelicts feel for one another, which they threaten to rescind if one of them seems able to move along to a life of success. Then the warm feelings turn to hostility. Pity is a way of keeping another derelict down with you. I fled from the idea of making common cause, making community, with other disabled people. And I've felt that same instinct from other disabled people I've met, such as Geoff Ward, who had polio about the same time I did and who is perhaps the best biographer of FDR. Geoff is friendly, but he doesn't seek enduring friendship on the basis of our common disability.

Whenever I encountered the novelist Wilfrid Sheed, who also had polio back then, I saw him instinctively draw back from me, before he knew anything about me — just seeing my crutches. I know the look when I see it; I give it to others.

At some extreme point, when I thought I myself was in danger of suffocation by fellow outcasts, I could identify with the remarks of another survivor, Lorenzo Milam: "I have to protect myself from the cripples all around me, who are my mirror image and who, at all times, are falling, puking, muling, slipping, spinning, wheedling, pulling, hanging on, all about me, trying to pull me down with them. My brothers! I stand apart from you: you, and your wasted limbs, your blighted breath, your palsy and your lordosis. I could care less about your sob stories."

In Alan Peshkin's European history course, Dave Grinstead and I, since we knew everything, spent the class periods being obnoxious. Mr. Peshkin very quickly hit on a tactic to correct this. He kept us after school and said he knew that we had already read everything he would be teaching but that others, some of them no less smart than we were, hadn't read those books or thought about that material yet and we shouldn't deprive them of an opportunity we had had. He would make a deal with us: If we would be useful in his class, remember that we didn't know absolutely everything quite yet, and take part in the group discussions in a civil manner, he would conduct seminars once a week in his own home for Dave and me and one or two others, where we could talk about history and philosophy and politics and see how smart we really were.

I remember one night that we were at Mr. Peshkin's house, Dave and I, and I think maybe Steve Hoffman was there, and we were talking about various rights of speech and thought. And Mr. Peshkin, our very own sly Socrates, asked if we thought we had the right to be poor, and, of course, privileged middle-class youths that we were, never having seen a right we didn't like, we said yes. And we were debating this right to be poor, with great eloquence, when Mr. Lombardo, the high school Spanish teacher, dropped by the house. Mr. Lombardo, who was from South America, had been dirt poor; and he laced into this group of privileged middle-class white boys with the passion and pain of his whole life. Having silenced us, shamed us, with this dose of reality, he went on to argue for the right not to be poor. He persuaded me.

Sometimes this heady stuff got me in the same kind of trouble as placing a toilet bowl at the entrance of the American Can Company. My teacher for American history was M. Annette Sheel. She was rightly regarded as one of the two or three finest teachers in the high school. (She deserves the lion's share of the credit for nurturing the interests of Kit Lasch, a few years older than I, who grew up to write *The Culture of Narcissism, Haven in a Heartless World,* and *The Revolt of the Elites,* among other books.) She was a constant pest about footnoting the history papers we handed in, returning most papers with the repeated query after one sentence and another, "What is your source?"

I decided to write a paper on Soviet–American relations, a topic of moderately lively interest at the time, since many of us thought we might be incinerated in a nuclear war at any moment. I went back to World War I and traced what "pattern" I thought I could find in the way Americans and Russians dealt with one another diplomatically. As it happened, Premier Nicolai Bulganin had recently proposed a "friendship treaty" between the United States and the Soviet Union, and the Eisenhower administration had turned it down — not once but twice. As a minor point toward the end of my paper, I stated that it would probably not be proposed a third time. And I no sooner set down the sentence than I could see the query coming from Miss Sheel: "What is your source?"

So I picked up the phone to call Premier Bulganin at the Kremlin. I remember saying to the operator in Barrington — in those days you picked up your receiver and an operator said, "Number, please" — "I want to speak to Premier Nicolai Bulganin at the Kremlin in Moscow."

The operator said, "How do you spell that?"

I said, "B-U-L-G . . ."

"No," the operator said, "the other one."

"Oh," I said. "M-O-S-C-O-W."

"Thank you," she said. "Please hold."

It turned out she could not put the call through right away, but she would put it through in the morning. That night I told Jim I was waiting for a call back from Bulganin, and he said he wanted to be there for it. Bets was away, and my parents had gone down to Chicago with friends to see a play that night, the first time they had left me alone since I'd returned from the hospital. They were extremely anxious about whether I would be all right on my own, and they made a big deal about giving me all their phone numbers at their hotel and the theater lobby and the restaurant where they were going to dinner.

Jim came over the next morning, and so did a couple of other friends, including Steve Hoffman, whom Jim told about the call, so there were four of us clustered around the two phones in the house.

The call went through. Someone said something in Russian. And I asked to speak to Premier Bulganin.

Some Russian was spoken in the background; there was evidently much confusion.

At last, an English-speaking person came on the line and asked who was calling. I identified myself.

And why was I calling? I explained the whole thing, and he asked me to wait.

Another voice came on the phone, a man with a heavy Russian accent, saying "hello." I identified myself and said I was writing a paper on Soviet foreign policy and I was concluding that the Russians would not offer their friendship treaty to the United States for a third time. Would the Russians offer the treaty again?

There was a silence at the other end.

Then after a few moments, the heavily accented voice said, "No."

I thanked him and said, "Do svidaniia."

He chuckled and said, "Do svidaniia."

And we hung up. Of course, I didn't know who it was I talked to.

Jim and the others began to yell in triumph, and I was confused. It hadn't occurred to me that this was an enormous prank. I thought it was naughty and smart, but they were wild with joy. They asked me what "do svidaniia" meant, and I said it was a word Alan Peshkin had taught me; it meant "goodbye."

They knew I meant to use this conversation as a footnote for my paper, but Jim said Miss Sheel would never believe I'd actually made the call. There was much conversation about this, and then Jim said he had a friend who had a friend who was a reporter at the *Chicago Tribune*. He would call this reporter, tell him about it, and the reporter could check it out and print a little item on page 16 or 32 or somewhere in the back of the paper, and that would prove it.

We called, and the reporter asked me a few questions.

When we got to school and told everyone what we had done, no one believed it. So I bet each of the doubters $5. When the phone bill finally came, the call cost $15. I had taken $25 worth of bets. I made $10 free and clear.

The day after the call, the story appeared on page one of the *Chicago Tribune,* and on page one of papers in London, Paris, Tokyo, Hong Kong, Guam, everywhere. According to the *Denver Post,* "a history student, [deciding] to write a term paper on Russia's latest overtures for a friendship treaty, really got to the bottom of things." Jim was quoted in the *Chicago Daily News* as saying that since it had been so easy to get Bulganin, we might try calling President Eisenhower next. On television, the Huntley–Brinkley news hour used it as their last, cute story of the night. (Several months later, the *Tribune* called to follow up on the story and reported the grade I got on the paper: A–. Miss Sheel remained hard to impress.)

As it happened, on the day the story hit the papers I was out of town with the exhibition square dance team. When we returned, we found the front of the school was mobbed by newspaper reporters and television cameramen. Reporters came rushing at me. Having seen this sort of thing on television myself, I knew how to behave. I pretended I was late for a very important meeting and made my way purposefully toward the front door of the school, answering the occasional question along the way. Someone asked me: "Where did you learn the Russian word for goodbye?" From one of my history teachers, I said. Who was that? Alan Peshkin.

I was met at the front door by the principal of the school, who stepped just outside the door, raised his hand so that all the television cameras could see that he was barring me from entering the building, and said, "You are expelled."

"What?" I said, really completely bewildered, wondering what terrible thing had happened.

"You are expelled."

"For what?"

"Never mind the reason," he said. "Get out."

And then I knew: He was terrified that the entire school, all its faculty, even the principal himself, might be considered Communists because I had called Bulganin.

That night the phone rang. Alan Peshkin was on the other end, speaking in hushed tones. "Why did you tell them I taught you how to speak Russian?"

I'd thought there was nothing wrong with it. Indeed, I thought he would be proud of having taught me.

"Don't ever mention my name again," he said, and hung up.

My parents, meanwhile, driving back from Chicago, heard the story on the car radio. They couldn't keep themselves from laughing when they came into the house. They had been worried I wouldn't know how to call Chicago.

I told my father that I'd been expelled.

"From where?" he asked incredulously. "From school?"

I told him what had happened. He was amazed. He went immediately to the phone and called his old friend Frank Thomas, the Superintendent of Schools and thus the boss of the principal. Frank agreed with my father that of course my being expelled was absurd; I should come to school the next morning; everything would be fine.

I had forgotten that I was living in the fifties, the height of the Cold War, when people were afraid of Communists, and the atmosphere in the country had made people afraid to be thought of as Communists or friends of Communists or even as people who knew how to speak Russian. Obviously, Alan Peshkin was afraid he was going to be fired, as perhaps he might have been in a school not run by Frank Thomas.

Some years later, I learned that the FBI was still keeping a file on me, a file they had started when, as a high school boy, in the loopy world of the fifties, I called Bulganin.

An FBI file: I was an official outsider.

twenty

When my father asked me whether I'd given any thought to where I might want to go to college, I said—because I'd picked up the idea from Bob Seaver—I thought I'd like to go to Harvard, and my father said, "I don't ever want to hear that word in this house again."

In my father's eyes, Harvard was not only a hotbed of Communism, it was also a center of godlessness and other sorts of irregularities. But what I'm sure weighed most heavily on his mind was that my wish to go to Harvard was a sign of my drift ever further into a world inside my head where he could never follow me, where he felt he would lose me forever.

Looking at a photograph of my father from this time, I see a man almost ten years younger than I am now. What a different life he led: thirty-five years in the world of Commonwealth Edison, making his way up the corporate hierarchy, secure in his job and his world, knowing that he could build an entire, good life within the culture of a prospering American business, a responsible and dependable man who, over and over in his conversation, would use the word "prudent" as an expression of high praise. A man who could be counted on in his work, and in his family. He was a distinguished- and gentle- and kind-looking man, with a calm, direct, but soft gaze; dark hair, neatly combed and parted high, with great splashes of silver at the temples; a charcoal gray suit with a white linen handkerchief in the breast pocket, a white shirt, French cuffs and silver filigree cufflinks, a silk rep stripe tie, highly polished black wing tips. He is a man who belongs to the world he lives in; for all his own anxieties, his own ability to erupt in frustration and rage, he is a man centered in the world he lives in, at ease, comfortable with it, liking the conventions of his time. In best-selling books of the day— *The Lonely Crowd, The Organization Man, The Man in the Gray Flannel Suit*— the white-collar executive was seen as a man alienated from his bureaucratic organization, discontented with his lot in the sphere of American business, feeling he lived a pointless existence, shuttling back and forth to work, comfortable in the material goods his career had brought to him and his family but lonely and lost in a life without any deeper meaning. My father felt none of this.

In the years to come, he would loosen his clasp on some of his beliefs; he would come to be less trusting of the announced aspirations of his favorite Republicans, less trusting of a political class that took the country into the Vietnam War, less trusting even of the unexamined intentions and effects of American business, more responsive to his own compassion for those less fortunate than he. He was a good man.

He didn't know how to reach out to me and bring me back as I drifted further and further away from him, but I believe he felt that the one place where he knew the terrain was Catholicism, which he viewed as the core of his life, and from which he sensed I was more and more distant. It was one place where he knew how to get some help.

He asked me if I would go and talk with a Jesuit priest he

knew, the head of a Jesuit monastery in the countryside near Barrington. And I agreed to go. I drove out to the monastery on my own one evening. The priest came to the door. He seemed to be alone in the monastery, it was that quiet. He took me through a dimly lit corridor to his study, a spacious room filled with books and warmed by a big fire in the fire-place. With not much in the way of preliminaries, he got directly to the point: What was the trouble? I hesitated. I didn't think I had any trouble; it was my father who was troubled because I was slipping away from the Catholic church. But I decided to accept the priest's construction of it, and I said, "I'm afraid I've lost my faith."

"What does that mean, to lose your faith? Often we find there are some points of dogma on which we have some reservations, or we are confused for a time, or angry."

"No, I don't think any of these is what I mean. I mean I've lost my faith. I no longer believe in God."

"I see," the priest said. And then he made a mistake. Instead of honoring my thoughts and feelings—instead of gently exploring the anger that had taken me to this place I was in—he decided to bully me, to intimidate me back into the church with his superior reasoning.

"If there is no God," he said, "where do you think we come from?"

I recognized immediately where *he* was coming from: this was the first of St. Thomas Aquinas's five proofs for the existence of God in his *Summa Theologica*. I had read the *Summa Theologica* and the *Summa Contra Gentiles*, as well as a lot of commentary on both, and some very recent refutations.

I said, I understood that every Effect has a Cause, and that we did not spring ex nihilo into life, but that, in searching back for an Uncaused Cause, as he seemed to be tending toward, I saw no reason, once we arrived back at the first atom, to take a leap suddenly to a spiritual plane in order to identify an Uncaused Cause, to require the physical universe to be contained by a spiritual universe rather than by its own skin. Why was not the hypothetical first atom an Uncaused Cause as well as God?

And, in any case, I said, wasn't the entire argument about an Uncaused Cause an immense tautology? Wasn't the end of the argument simply assumed in the premises of its beginning?

He was taken aback. Whether or not I was as smart as I thought I was, clearly I was not going to be easy to persuade.

Nonetheless, because he was a Jesuit, he was not without resources; and he moved swiftly to Aquinas's second and third proofs.

I tried to look relaxed and spontaneous, as though his remarks had never occurred to me before, as though I had never read Aquinas but was simply engaging in the conversation as he framed it. But I felt like a chess master. The priest moved time after time exactly where I knew he was going to move, and—as it turned out!—he had not read as much as I had.

We spent an hour at it; by the end he was red-faced and angry. At last, he said, "Well, I'm afraid there is nothing I can do for you."

I thanked him for trying, and as he escorted me back to the door, I wondered: Am I trying to induce frustration and anger in others just because I feel it myself? Am I trying to make this priest feel as bad as I felt when I was given extreme unction? Is this my version of giving extreme unction to him? Have I come to such a state that I'm now using conversation as a form of revenge? Yes, I thought, I have: This *was* vengeance, and, really, it felt good to me and made me want to cry out, as my pulse went racing, "Yes. Yes. I scored! I scored!" at the same time that it felt bad and wrong and filled me with a sense of guilt and shame. And then I calmed down; I thought, after all, I shouldn't feel too guilty; he used knowledge as a weapon to bully *me*. He was a grown-up. He was the one who wasn't supposed to behave like this. I just out-Jesuited him a little bit.

That was the end of church for me, and the end of much else. In the summer, at a garden party at the home of some friends of my parents, where Big Chuck Buckley stood next to the outdoor grill with spatula in hand, wearing an apron and a chef's hat, I could still stand—holding both crutch and cane in one hand, leaving my other hand free to hold a Scotch and water—and talk about football and the economy, the rise and fall of the Dow Jones, the best route to drive from Barrington to the golf club in Lake Forest or Park Ridge; I could talk about the prospects for the Chicago White Sox in the pennant race or for the Chicago Bears in the coming football season, but I was out of there. Among these good, friendly, generous people, I could perform the role of my father's son, but I couldn't live it.

The psychologist Erik Erikson, in his book *Young Man Luther*, wrote of the once-born and the twice-born: The once-born grow up secure in their families and the world their families inhabit and mature seamlessly into that same world; the twice-born find, no matter what they might wish, that at some point, they no longer belong to the lives into which they were born. They must fly to another world.

And I did. Even now, whenever I return to the Midwest, coming in to O'Hare, getting off the plane, being met by a friend to drive me out toward Barrington, the moment I sense the contours of the rolling hills, the quality of the light in the late afternoon, the thick, low-hanging clouds of late November, Thanksgiving time, I am overcome with a sense of well-being, of being home—as though I had been imprinted by it, like a gosling or a duckling, that instinct of knowing the place I come from, where I am now, forever, an outsider. The football letter sweater, the robust good cheer of the cocktail hour, the game on television, the tweed jacket, the gray flannel trousers, the hand-knit argyle socks, the red and green plaid Pendleton shirt, the cashmere pullover, the Irish setter stretched out on the carpet, friends coming by, the goodness of intentions, the deep pleasure in things as they are, the acceptance of the world, the gratitude for the given order of things, the company of the well-adjusted: the world I longed for and left.

That world is gone now, entirely. As it turns out, even as I was leaving it, it was disappearing. The fifties, that time of the warm nuclear family gathered around the fireplace after Thanksgiving, the sense of a safe, secure order that would never end, of social structures and aspirations and politicians and patriarchal figures you could count on—all this was dissolving into a world more complex and difficult and contradictory: it came to seem, finally, that my own life and the life of my times could be described in the same words. We have both come to embrace a different life.

By the time I was leaving for college, polio was a thing of the past. It had been only a few months before the junior prom that the National Foundation for Infantile Paralysis had at last geared up for its large-scale field trial of a polio vaccine, administered from April through June, 1954. They needed 1.8 million children, spread across the United States, to take part in the test. They needed to find places where polio was likely to break out and where the public health services were competent enough to administer the vaccine and keep records. The trial required more than 300,000 volunteer workers: 20,000 doctors, 40,000 nurses, 50,000 teachers, 200,000 lay volunteers. It was, as Jane Smith wrote, "the largest field trial ever held, the greatest peacetime mobilization of civilians in American history, and the most eagerly observed and heavily publicized scientific program until the space launches a decade later. . . . Privately funded, privately organized and supervised . . . the development and testing of the Salk vaccine was in many ways a crowning example of democratic self-help."

It was, said the *New York Times,* "a turning point in medical history. Gone are the old helplessness, the fear of an invisible enemy, the frustration of physicians. Gone, too, are the 'iron lungs' in which the paralyzed languished, and gone the hot-weather epidemics of poliomyelitis. Science has enriched mankind with one of its finest gifts."

According to the *Minneapolis Tribune*'s science writer Victor Cohn, "The development of polio vaccines, present and future, is a monument to several important things. To initiative and individualism, and to willing cooperation. To the spirit of starting things, and of getting things done. To the American volunteer — 'the guy who pitches in.' "

"The scientific atmosphere of the 1950s," as Allan Brandt would later write in the *International Journal of Health Sciences,* "was fraught with Cold War overtones. The vaccine, an affirmation of American scientific and technological progress, was viewed as a triumph of the American system. American

science, pragmatic and purposeful, demonstrated the continued viability of the promise of American life."

Eleanor Roosevelt went out to Franklin's grave and placed
a wreath there. The *Seattle Post-Intelligencer* sent a reporter out
to the Northwest Respirator Center, where Dorothy Baldwin,
age twenty-five, lying in an iron lung, said, "It came too late
for me, but thank God it comes in time for my children!"

Salk had become a great American hero, one of the great
heroes of the twentieth century; indeed, he stands as almost
the last of unsullied American heroes. Of course, because he
was pushy, because he went along with the hasty National
Foundation test of the vaccine, because some disagreed with
his science and with the ultimate worth of the dead-virus vaccine, because he seemed, with all his radio appearances and the
newspaper articles about him, a publicity hound, the polio research scientists regarded him with even greater contempt
than before. He was not given the Nobel Prize; that went to
Enders and Weller and Robbins, the pure scientists. He was
never invited to join the National Academy of Sciences. When
Albert Sabin came out with his live-virus vaccine in 1961, the
Salk vaccine faded from universal use. (Both vaccines are used
today, under different circumstances. Though the live-virus
Sabin vaccine carries a minuscule risk of causing polio, it is
more widely used because of its ease of administration and its
long-lasting effects. The really cautious parents will have their
children get the ultra-safe Salk vaccine first and then, with that
immunity established, add the Sabin vaccine for the long-term
protection.)

Still, Salk remains a great popular hero, a perfect exemplar
of a time when Americans believed that money and science

and sheer will could solve anything. Indeed, Salk not only grew out of this culture, but, in his success, he contributed to the illusion that smart, determined men could declare war on any problem and solve it: the war in Vietnam, the war on poverty, the war on cancer. It has taken us decades to learn that the world is more complex than the wonderful Dr. Salk and his colleagues and celebrants made it appear. How much different and more refreshingly naive and trusting those times were can be seen in a single phenomenon: Were people reluctant to come forward to be injected with an unknown vaccine that, some said, would *give* them polio? On the contrary— such was the trust in scientists and experts and leaders, and in the benevolence of public enterprises of all kinds, that the contributors to the March of Dimes begged to be guinea pigs: children and parents clamored to be given the untested vaccine. And, after all the data was sorted out, even the most skeptical had to admit: The vaccine worked. There had been 58,000 new cases of polio in 1952. By 1957, there were 5,000. By 1960, there were only 3,000. And in the United States today, as Jane Smith has said, "a child is more likely to be struck by lightning than by polio."

When I came out of the subway into Harvard Square and saw the wrought-iron gates at the entrance to Harvard College, I felt I had been delivered at last into a world that valued, above everything else, the life of the mind; a world where, for me, the playing field was level.

Of course, I was among people who wanted to become businessmen and drink martinis and cheer at football games. I myself, still a boy of the Midwest, wanted to drink martinis and cheer at football games, too. But I was among people who also loved what I loved, among people who loved books and all the life they contained.

I was on my way into a world of history and archaeology and painting and sculpture, of words and sentences, a world where people were consumed by an interest in bits of painted pottery from digs in the desert, by Matisse's sybaritic paintings of his life in the Mediterranean town of Collioure, the gnarled and twisted worlds of Bruegel and Bosch, the rich, intricate human landscapes of Shakespeare and Dickens and my old Greeks; a world where I would meet people who had given their lives to deciphering ancient hieroglyphs or understanding the life of Samuel Johnson; a world where I lost consciousness of my body entirely, where the pleasures were inexhaustible, where I was able to share a life with others on equal footing, roam the world with them freely as equal companions, limited by nothing but our thoughts and passions.

And so when I walked through the gate into Harvard Yard, I felt nothing so much as relief, and my entire body relaxed, as it had not since Mrs. Fuller had said, "This boy has polio."

epilogue

Now, more than forty years later, I am not quite as steady on my feet as I was when I first went off to Harvard. I am beginning to lose a little strength in my right shoulder, and a little something in the grip of my right hand. My left arm and hand, so little affected by the polio when it first struck, remain my most dependable aides. Taking stock in front of a mirror: Well, let's face it, I'm sixty years old. My hair is getting ever more gray, just as my father's did. I weigh 140 pounds, exactly what I weighed when I left home for college, but my muscle tone is not what it once was. My skin is not as smooth. I am a little less than the six feet tall I used to be. My arms and shoulders still look strong, the legs are still skinny, the left foot still displays the telltale drop. This body has been dragged through life, and it shows some damage.

During the winter, I wear flannel shirts; in the summer, polo shirts—shirts that are not so bulky that they will grab hold of a crutch and throw me to the ground but that are generous enough to let my arms and shoulders move easily inside them. I wear khaki pants—lightweight. I don't carry extra weight. My high-risk item: cuffs at the bottoms of the khakis—dangerous things that might reach out and take hold of a crutch tip. But we all have to take some chances for the sake of fashion.

In fall, winter, and spring, and even on cold summer nights, I wear the same lightweight red ski jacket. Snug at the waist so it doesn't get in the way of crutch or cane. I wear red Converse hightop sneakers, which others take as a happening fashion statement while I secretly treasure them, too, because they are lightweight, grip the ground well, and keep that left toe from dropping too far toward the pavement. I wear this costume all the time, for formal and casual wear. I see how people look at me, thinking me agreeably relaxed or unaccountably eccentric. I think of myself as a practical person.

I walk still with a worn wooden cane in my left hand and a fire-engine-red Canadian crutch in my right hand. I can walk for blocks at a time. I can stroll through a museum, staying on my feet for several hours at a time. I enjoy the smooth paths of a city park. I like that part of the beach just above the reach of the last tongues of the waves where the sand is hard and smooth. I can go to movies. I can take taxis. I can fly to Paris. I can spend hours in a restaurant talking over dinner. I can read. I can write. I can sail. I can swim. I can make love.

Of course, my recovery from polio in high school—coming back from being in bed unable to move, recovering an ability to move my hands and arms and to stand on my own feet, going to basketball games and the junior prom on crutches, figuring out that I would need to rely not on my body but on my head in order to make my way in the world, setting out on a course of reading and then of college that would take me at last to a life in the world that was self-sufficient and independent—as crucial as it was to me, was not the end of the story.

In the years after college, I threw myself into life with an urge to have all of it that I could. Simply proving that I could return to high school and get through college was not enough. As Leonard Kriegel wrote of his own recovery from polio, "The man who is 'successful' at creating a life out of the after-effects of disease . . . discovers that he must sooner or later fight against an inflated notion of what it is he has achieved. When a mutual friend praised Franz Rosenzweig's courage in living with the pain and suffering inflicted on him by a long struggle with cancer, Freud, doomed to undergo the same long struggle, is reported to have said, 'What else can he do?'"

At a certain point, as Kriegel says, "What seems to me to have happened . . . was an almost instinctive recognition that I had to will myself into being, that I had to kind of will a self, to create a self. And I think that's the *one* gift, if that's the word, that one can take from polio, or from a disease like it. What I wanted, above all else, was to be able to define who I was . . . and . . . what I finally realized was that I wanted to live on my own terms . . . but that I'd also do the things I'd been told I couldn't do, like I would *travel,* I would marry, I would have children, I would—you know—live."

But each recovery we make in life only reveals the next complication behind it. As Arnold Beisser has written, his "relationship" with his disability evolved, not unlike a marriage. Beisser thought the last stage of his recovery was "surrendering with dignity and grace, or embracing the new life" as though he had chosen it. But then he discovered that this "last" stage was "not necessarily either final or complete." One does not achieve grace and then live forever after on a serene, unchanging glide path of bliss. Life continues to change. New things surface; old wounds hidden by bigger wounds show up when the bigger wounds are healed; new clusters of misgivings and confusion take shape to replace old clusters of exhausted adjustments. New things come along to be accepted with grace and peace. The disability and its challenges continue to evolve, and one must achieve acceptance and grace and peace again and again, day after day.

Then, too, all this thinking about recovery and about the self—this obsessive concern with how *I* was doing—was itself disabling. Feeling the need to prove myself in my twenties, pursuing quick, striking success as a young editor of a magazine of history and the arts, preoccupied by my own urges and insecurities and compensatory strategies, the prey of my own unexamined fears and confusions and rages, savaging my own body with alcohol and drugs, feeling unlovable and unloved, I was not a good partner in life.

Physical damage is easy to repair; the psyche takes longer. In my case, it also took years of heavy drinking, some drugs, a fall into very deep depression, the love of more than one woman, three failed marriages, a passionate life of writing history books that finally seemed pointless in their pretense that it is possible to speak dispassionately about what life is and how it unfolds, finding my true self at last in the plays that I write, in another love, and in the constant love of my children.

And, along with drinking and depression and failed marriages, I've had a great deal of the pleasures of normal life, of family life, of the happiness as well as the difficulties of marriage, the pleasures of children, of vacations in rented country houses, of going to the theater and concerts, of travel in the world. I've had three lives or more in the space of one: For some years I was the editor of a magazine of art and history and archaeology and literature and the other liberal arts; and then for some years I paid the rent and sent children to college by writing books of American diplomatic and political history; and now I have a life in the theater, writing plays and taking the train up from New York to Brown University a couple of days a week to teach playwriting.

I tell my students: I like plays that are not too neat, too finished, too presentable. My own plays are broken, jagged, filled with sharp edges, filled with things that take sudden turns, career into each other, smash up, veer off in sickening turns. That feels good to me. It feels like my life. And then I like to put this chaotic stuff—with some sense of struggle remaining—into a classical form, a Greek form, or a beautiful dance theater piece, or some other effort at civilization.

Recently, I have come again and again to take the text of a classic Greek play, smash it to ruins, and then, atop its ruined structure of plot and character, write a new play, with all-new language, characters of today speaking like people of today, set in the America of my time—so that America today lies, as it were, in a bed of ancient ruins. Plays filled with song, dance, movement, beauty, heartache, a world that feels good, exciting, real, familiar, like home, like the high drama that life really is, like the real world, plays in which I know that I come at last to feel not the insistence of some standard of normality, but rather the true acceptance of life, and of the grace and peace that follow from that. The Greeks took no easy problems. They put on the stage a world of unspeakable anguish, of matricide and fratricide and patricide, and then they refused to blink. They looked into the abyss of human life and human nature with open eyes and understood that the thing to do is to feel life as it is, in all its anguish as well as its aspirations, its missed opportunities and its savored beauties, never to falsify it, never to pretty it up; but rather to look at it bravely, unflinchingly. In the sheer steadiness and clarity and courage of that gaze will you achieve real understanding of the complexity of life; and from that come acceptance, grace, and enduring peace. The greatest blessing you can have in life is to live long enough to take it in.

My own feeling of acceptance and peace came finally, I think, from the Greeks, but it took me more than forty years after Maude Strouss's gift of Plato to understand it.

These days, wherever I am, as I make my way down the street with a crutch and a cane, I am taken as a natural friend by every derelict on the street. Every bum in New York says hello to me. I'm hardly ever asked for money, and then only as a peer. Often I stop and chat. On some streets, I have regular friends. In fact, all outsiders automatically consider me one of their own—all those who live, in one way or another, on the margins. And it's true. I am one of their own. We share some kinds of knowledge and feelings that don't need to be spoken; we understand one another with a look, a moment of stopping and connecting with one another's eyes. We feel comfortable with each other; I'm grateful to be among their company. All over the world, I am recognized as an insider by the outsiders. So I feel at home in the world.

True enough, when I walk down the street I need to watch my feet on the sidewalk to make sure I don't trip and fall; I can't look too much at the landscape, or the other people on the street—and that cuts me off a little from the world. And when I am standing and talking to someone, if I need to shift my weight to keep standing it takes that much extra concentration in addition to giving full attention to what another person is saying. This is why old people "forget"—because they never heard it the first time, because they can't hear or because they were trying to concentrate on not falling down while it was being said to them. And this is why sitting in a café with a friend or two is, for me, as it was for my father in his later years, one of the best ways I have of being out in the world. I can forget my body, the way other people do most of the time. I'm smarter sitting down than I am standing up.

I'm told by people who have had a leg amputated that it takes years for their nervous system to recognize the absence of the leg. The leg might be gone from the hip down, but the foot still itches, or the knee hurts. And this phantom limb diminishes only gradually over time before finally disappearing. For myself, to this day I have never had a dream in which I walked with crutches; I've never had a dream in which I was disabled in any way; in my dreams my body is as intact as it was when I was fourteen. I can't often take the time, but when I can, I love to sleep ten hours a night, sometimes more, and catch some extra dreams.

I still have moments of frustration and anger. I find it constantly amazing that after all these years on crutches, they still don't seem natural to me; my inner sense of what is normal is still what it was when I was fourteen. The expectations of what it will be to have a normal life are embedded so early in life, and so deep. In some senses, I haven't adjusted a bit. And I am still followed always by my shadow self, the boy who was overcome by polio, undone by it, enraged by it, exhausted by it, who wants to give up. This boy, full of complaints and irritations, too tired to go on, too overwhelmed by the difficulties, resentful of the unfairness of it, too angry at being unable to run up stairs or play basketball with his kids, envious of others, bitter, frightened, this boy sometimes still wants to quit. And there are still days when I have to talk him into going on, sometimes several times a day.

In truth, the victory of Salk and Sabin over polio was incomplete and prematurely announced, too. In the United States, polio had nearly disappeared by 1960, and it was eradicated in most of the industrialized world soon after that. But it raged on in the rest of the world—there have been millions of cases in the past several decades. In 1988 the World Health Organization announced a campaign to eliminate polio by the year 2000. In 1995, more than 80 million children were immunized in China in a single day; more than 300 million children were immunized that year in fifty-one different countries. And it now looks as though the World Health Organization will meet its target of eliminating the last vestiges of polio within a few years of the year 2000. Today, there are perhaps 300,000 or 400,000 polio survivors still living in the United States, and probably more than 10 million in the rest of the world.

A few years ago, when I was making a cup of tea in the kitchen one day, I fell suddenly to the floor and broke my knee. I couldn't quite understand what had happened. I had only turned slightly—as I did a dozen times a day—while I was standing at the kitchen counter. And yet it seemed that my whole delicately rigged system of compensatory muscles and balancing maneuvers had given way all together. I went down like a sack of rocks.

As I soon learned, this event was the announcement of post-polio syndrome, a gradual loss of strength that begins thirty or forty years after the original onslaught of polio, this time in slow motion—and with a cause, and an end, that no one knows.

Those who were the first to experience it some years ago were told by their doctors that it was just a normal sign of aging, or that it was psychosomatic, or—when the symptoms seemed undeniably serious—that it might be amyotrophic lateral sclerosis (Lou Gehrig's disease). Polio survivors who had recovered so well from their polio that they hiked and climbed mountains without crutches or canes would notice that they had begun to need a cane for balance or that their knees would buckle and they would fall or that they could no longer go up stairs without a railing to hold on to, that they limped, that they needed a walker, or a wheelchair, that they were so exhausted they couldn't get out of bed. Clearly, something was happening beyond ordinary aging—though the common loss of strength with age intensified the phenomenon. Those who have had polio have already lost a good measure of their strength; they are already operating on the margins, so that when a share of that margin is diminished, the effect can be dramatic.

A number of theories about post-polio syndrome have been proposed. Some people have said that the polio virus lies dormant in the system for years and then flares again, like the chicken pox virus that sometimes returns as shingles. Some people have thought that the strain polio survivors place on compensatory muscles that were designed for some other or lesser use finally becomes too great, and the overburdened muscles begin to give out after years of overuse. Some people have speculated that the nerve fibers themselves, those that were not killed by polio, responded to increased demand by growing additional nerve endings, and that finally this additional strain on the very structure of the nerves caused them to quit.

Here are the symptoms: excessive, chronic fatigue, sometimes profound, sometimes lasting for days or weeks; new pain in joints and muscles, sometimes low-level, sometimes intense, often lasting for months at a time; reduced endurance; new breathing difficulties; intolerance to cold accompanied by burning pain; the slow ebbing of strength.

Once again, I began to listen to the stories of others, to wonder how I compare.

Rosemary Marx, who had polio in 1946 at age three, recovered so well that she could swim and run and play softball and ride horses, and she grew up to be a nurse, accustomed to working long hours, until more than forty years after she had recovered from her illness, when she began to limp. She was overcome by exhaustion from time to time so that she had to lie down. She noticed fatigue in her voice. She began to have swallowing difficulties. She felt she could never catch up on her sleep. In order to continue working, she went in for physical therapy to try to build back some strength. But the exercises, by adding stress to her muscles, only made her condition worse. The muscle weakness increased until she had to stop working. She was denied Social Security disability benefits and had to hire a lawyer to appear before a judge on her behalf. She felt guilty, she said, about not working, and she was in considerable pain, and now she felt she had to beg for help. In suing for her Social Security benefits, she was required to file a document confirming that she was "permanently disabled"—the first time she had ever had to say that about herself. And, for the first time in all those forty years, she said, she cried.

Jennifer Williams, who had polio in 1949, when she was two years old, recovered so thoroughly that she never needed braces or crutches, never needed therapy as a child. Although she had some difficulties with residual weakness, mostly in her back, she grew up to live an active life and raise four children. And then, in the early 1980s, she and her family moved into a larger house, with a garden and fruit trees—more rooms to clean, more yardwork. And she began to get weaker and weaker every day, finally switching from a cane to a wheelchair.

Grace Audet, who had polio in 1952 at age eight, commenced some twenty-five or thirty years afterward to come down with bronchial infections every fall and to wonder "Why can't I keep going?" She thought her low energy might be the result of inactivity, and so she began a regime of exercise, only to find she was getting worse. When at last she was told she had post-polio syndrome, she said she was relieved, because "when you look as healthy as I looked, there's a tendency for people to think that this is all in your head, that you're a hypochondriac." Several years ago, she started to wear a leg brace.

I hear stories like these, and I wonder: What are the odds? So far, of those Americans who had polio, 40 to 50 percent have developed post-polio syndrome. Let's make that *only* 40 to 50 percent. Of those, not all have taken to wheelchairs. The syndrome, like polio itself, strikes with varying intensity: some seem to get off with only a little loss of strength, and that only very slowly, over a long period of time. Maybe this time I am going to be one of the lucky ones again.

Still, one day not long ago, when I went to the Strand, New York's best secondhand bookstore—really the only bookstore left that is at all like the shops Alan Peshkin used to take me to in high school—I went down into the basement where the collection of American history books is kept. I hadn't been down in this part of the Strand for more than a year. At one time I had been accustomed to go there at least once or twice a month and come away with four or five books in my hands. I rooted around for a while and found two books I had to have. And then, returning to the bottom of the steps back to the main floor, I realized that I could no longer swing myself easily up the stairs at the Strand. Even worse: Whereas, with my strong grip, I used to be able to hold two or even three books as well as my canes in each hand, now I felt the books slipping out of my hand. I could only manage one step at a time, and my toe caught on each step. One of the clerks offered to carry my books up to the cash register for me.

In that moment, I recognized that I had begun to move like my own father had when he was in his late eighties: with elaborate care, in slow motion, placing each foot, each cane tip, scrupulously, from lack of strength and from fear of falling. I stopped denying that I had been overtaken by post-polio syndrome. I began to notice other things. I no longer stand at the bathroom sink to shave; I lean against the sink for support. It occurs to me that I always reach with my left hand for a book on a high bookshelf; gradual weakening in my right shoulder makes it hard to lift my right hand above my head. I don't maintain my balance as well as I used to: if I need to step around a table or a chair in a restaurant, I falter and bump into the backs of chairs and the edges of tables. If I try to walk more than ten or twelve blocks, I find I have to be prepared to pay the price that the muscles in my arms will hurt badly for a week or two. In short, I'm discovering a whole new set of physical limitations, and I feel the old anger welling up. I have to say, I hate it.

But I also have to say, I think I can hate it and just get on with my life at the same time. With me, post-polio syndrome seems to be not so severe, and its progress seems fairly slow. And, let's face it, I've had a lot of practice at this sort of thing by now. I've come to see that sorrow and loss and regret and life and pleasure do not need to crowd one another out. And, really, this time around, this loss of powers seems not so much to set me apart from the rest of the world as to knit me in with others, with the aging that eventually overtakes us all. This is the common lot. And, I think I can contemplate it now with almost perfect equanimity—which is to say, with a fairly normal sense of dread and rage and bitterness and frenzy and despair at the prospect of losing strength and dying—and go on to luxuriate in the present. I'm glad to notice that I feel such a longing for life.

I'm in love with Laurie. We are living together in an old brownstone with a garden in the back of the house. I write at home at a desk in a little room just off the kitchen, a cup of tea always close at hand. On my bookshelf as I write, within reach of my hand at this moment, is a copy of Plato's *Symposium;* on one shelf are a dozen history books that I have written; and somewhere here are the dozen plays I've written. On the wall to one side of my desk are framed photographs of scenes from my plays: a man standing amid burning ruins atop an upended bed, a man in a full-length wool khaki coat standing on a floor of open books, an old woman with a baby in her arms gazing out the window of an abandoned building, a woman in a blue satin slip dancing through a gold house made of sticks. Propped up just next to my desk lamp is a little framed note that my eldest daughter Erin, now thirty-five years old, wrote to me when she was a small child: "dear dad I love you oh Dear oh dear I love love love you, love From

Erin." On the wall just above the desk is a collage of photographs that my son Charles, now twenty-nine, made when he was in high school: photographs of the woods in autumn, inscribed with the legend ". . . and those castles made of sand melt into the sea, eventually." Elsewhere is a program from my young daughter Sarah's dance performance last year, when she was twelve, a dance of a girl with her violin that she choreographed herself; and, leaning against a few volumes of the classical tragedies of Eurpides, is a painting by my daughter Alice from last year when she was eight years old, a smiling face with sunglasses, floating in the sunny blue sky, surrounded by white clouds.

Laurie and I do some gardening. In the afternoons, we go out to Roberto's café and drink coffee and tea. We sleep through the night in each other's arms. We lie in bed in the morning in each other's arms. We hold each other a lot; we just hold each other. We make love a lot. I hope it lasts forever. Maybe by now I am able to forget myself and think of Laurie, of my children and my friends, set aside my own concerns as no longer the most interesting drama in the world, turn my feelings outward to embrace life. I am no longer interested in recovery or restitution. You don't recover from the events of life, you take them with you, you knit them in, you grow with them and around them; they become who you are; they are life itself; how else my life might have been is unknowable; and the truth is, I wouldn't change it for any other.

notes

I am greatly indebted to a number of other writers whose stories I've recounted in this book, and whose research on the history of polio I've used in narrating the background of my own story: most especially to Kathryn Black's *In the Shadow of Polio* (Addison Wesley Longman, 1996), in which she not only tells the story of her own mother's bout with polio, but also gives much of the social history of the times, of the experiences of other polio survivors, and of the stories of Salk and Sabin and the March of Dimes—all of which I have relied on for my account. For the history of polio, I relied also on Jane S. Smith's *Patenting the Sun: Polio and the Salk Vaccine* (Morrow, 1990) as well as John R. Paul's *History of Poliomyelitis* (Yale University Press, 1971). I'm also very deeply indebted to *Polio's Legacy: An Oral History* (University Press of America, 1996), edited by Edmund Sass, which contains many personal narratives that have informed my own text or that I've incorporated directly into it, including those of Robert Gurney, Richard Owen, Ray K. Gullickson, Marilynne Rogers, David Kangas, Kay Brutger, Gail Bias, Barb Johnson, Edmund Sass, Carole Sauer, Sharon Kimball, Len Jordan, Mary Ann Hoffman, Arvid Schwartz, Diane Keyser, June Radosovich, Evelyn Fink, Jeanne Molloy, Jack Dominik,

Charles A. Stone, and Bill Van Cleve. Several other narratives
I consulted constantly and used in part are Leonard Kriegel's
Falling into Life (North Point Press, 1991), Arnold R. Beisser's
Flying Without Wings (Doubleday, 1989), and Robert F. Hall's
Through the Storm: A Polio Story (North Star Press, 1990). I
am indebted, too, to Eric J. Cassell's *The Nature of Suffering*
(Oxford University Press, 1991); Fred Davis's *Passage
Through Crisis: Polio Victims and Their Families* (Bobbs-
Merrill, 1963); Howard Brody's *Stories of Sickness* (Yale
University Press, 1987); Arthur W. Frank's "Reclaiming an
Orphan Genre: The First-Person Narratives of Illness," in *Lit-
erature and Medicine,* vol. 13, no. 1, Spring 1994; Daniel J.
Wilson's "Covenants of Work and Grace: Themes of Recov-
ery and Redemption in Polio Narratives," in *Literature and
Medicine,* vol. 13, no. 1, Spring 1994; Peg Kehret's *Small
Steps: The Year I Got Polio* (Albert Whitman & Company,
1996); Naomi Rogers's *Dirt and Disease: Polio Before FDR*
(Rutgers University Press, 1992); Tony Gould's *Summer
Plague: Polio and Its Survivors* (Yale University Press, 1995);
W. T. Lhamon, Jr.'s *Deliberate Speed: The Origins of a Cul-
tural Style in the American 1950s* (Smithsonian Institution
Press, 1990); and Karal Ann Marling's *As Seen on TV: The Vi-
sual Culture of Everyday Life in the 1950s* (Harvard University
Press, 1994); as well as the deep resources of information,
magazine articles, personal stories, exchanges of chat, medical
histories, and anecdotes to be found at and through such Internet sites as the Polio Survivors' Page, The Rollin' Rat, and
Polio Information Center Online.

I have tried to acknowledge my sources for specific quota-
tions or other material as I went along in my narrative, but I
want to mention more especially that I am obliged in chapter

3 to Edmund Sass for a half-dozen of the stories of other children who had polio; in chapter 4 to Kathryn Black for her gathering of the stories that made the rounds at that time, and also to Smith for the stories about nuclear radiation and polio and "juice on the gourd," and to Gould for the stories about the football stars who committed suicide, the Hemlock drink, the iron lung made from a coffin, and the "Inner Sanctum" anecdote; in chapter 6, much of the material about show business figures in the polio campaign comes from Smith and Black; in chapter 7, the story of the Minneapolis boy comes from Sass; in chapter 8, the stories of Rogers, Kangas, Brutger, Van Cleve, Zahler, Kimball, and Johnson are from Sass; in chapter 9, Charlie's story is from Davis, the story about the D. T. Watson home is from Gould, the story of the boy who will be playing with the Little League is from Davis, and H. C. A. Lassen is quoted in Black; in chapter 10, Gurney's and Gullickson's stories appear in Sass's anthology; in chapter 12, all these stories of families' reactions to their children's prospects come from Davis; in chapter 14, I've relied on Lhamon for most of the material on American pop culture; in chapter 15, as I mentioned above, I've relied on Black and Smith, and on Gould, especially for some of the material about Sabin; in chapter 20, I relied again on Smith and Black for much of the history of the Salk vaccine; in the Epilogue, the stories of Marx, Williams, and Audet are from Sass.

acknowledgments

I'd like to acknowledge, with the greatest thanks, my debt to my agent, Lois Wallace, who made me write this book, and to my editor, Bill Phillips, whose unerring taste and judgment helped me to write it as well as I could, and to Laurie Williams, whose great instincts and advice inform every word.